Thinking Recursively

with *Java*

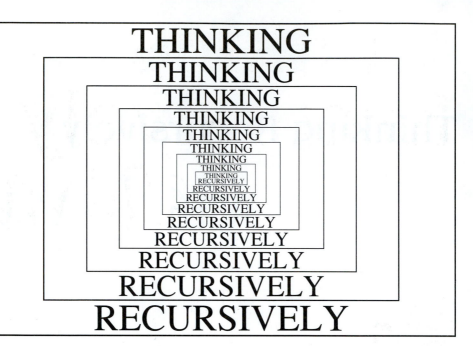

Thinking Recursively

with *Java*

ERIC ROBERTS
Department of Computer Science
Stanford University
Stanford, California

WILEY

PUBLISHER	Bruce Spatz
ACQUISITIONS EDITOR	Catherine Shultz
DEVELOPMENTAL EDITOR	Lauren Rusk
EDITORIAL ASSISTANT	Bridget Morrisey
MARKETING MANAGER	Phyllis Cerys
SENIOR PRODUCTION EDITOR	Ken Santor
COVER DESIGNER	Hope Miller

This book was set in Times Roman by Eric Roberts and printed and bound by Courier Westford. The cover was printed by Phoenix Color Corporation.

ISBN 13: 978-0-471-70146-0

ISBN 10: 0-471-70146-7

Printed in the United States of America

10 9 8 7 6 5 4 3 2 1

To Lauren

Loving you more and more each day.

Preface

When students first encounter recursion, they often react with suspicion to the entire idea, as if they have just been exposed to some conjurer's trick rather than a critically important programming methodology. That suspicion arises because recursion has few analogues in everyday life and requires students to think in an unfamiliar way. A few students catch on to the basic idea after a few examples. Many more, however, find the topic mysterious and frustrating for a long period of time. Immobilized by their initial failure to acquire the concept, all too many students never learn to apply recursive techniques and proceed to more advanced courses unable to write programs that depend on the use of recursive strategies.

To give students a more extensive introduction to this topic that they find so difficult, I wrote *Thinking Recursively* while I was teaching at Wellesley College in Massachusetts. John Wiley and Sons published the book as a supplementary text in 1986, and it has remained in print ever since, even though the rapid evolution of the field means that certain features of the book—most notably its use of Pascal as its programming language—make the original edition hard to use for today's courses. To celebrate the 20th anniversary of a book that has become something of a classic, John Wiley has commissioned this new edition in which Pascal has been replaced by Java.

The point of this book is to encourage students to "think recursively." Learning to think in this new way requires students to examine recursion from several different perspectives. Chapter 1 provides an informal overview of simple recursive examples outside the context of programming. Chapter 2 examines the fundamental mathematical concepts underlying recursion and helps the student develop an appropriate conceptual model. In particular, this chapter covers mathematical induction and computational complexity in considerable detail. This discussion is designed to be nonthreatening to students with mathematical anxiety and, at the same time, to include enough formal structure so that students understand the extent to which computer science depends on mathematics for its theoretical foundations.

Chapter 3 applies the technique of recursive decomposition to various mathematical functions and begins to show how recursion is represented in Pascal. Chapter 4 continues this discussion in the context of recursive procedures, emphasizing the parallel between recursive decomposition and the more familiar technique of stepwise refinement.

Chapters 5 through 9 then present several examples of the use of recursion to solve increasingly sophisticated problems. Chapter 7 covers recursive sorting techniques, illustrating the applicability of the recursion methodology to practical problem domains. Chapter 9 contains many delightful graphical examples, which make excellent exercises and demonstrations. The examples in the text are based on the **acm.graphics** package developed by the Java Task Force appointed by the Association of Computing Machinery (ACM). Although the packages provided by the Java Task Force make it much easier to use graphics at the introductory level, it should be easy to adapt this chapter to other libraries and tools.

Chapter 10 examines the use of recursive data structures and contains several important examples. Structurally, this chapter appears late in the text primarily to ensure that students have had a chance to understand the fundamentals of data structures before they try to master this material. If this book is used in an intermediate-level course in which students already have experience with data structures, it may be more appropriate to cover Chapter 10 immediately after Chapter 7.

Finally, Chapter 11 examines the underlying implementation of recursion. For some students, understanding the implementation is essential to developing the confidence they need to apply the "recursive leap of faith." There is, however, some danger in introducing this material too early. For many students, focusing on the details of the implementation may make it impossible to develop the essential holistic vision that recursive programming demands.

I am deeply grateful for the assistance of many people who have helped to shape the final form of the text. For this revised edition, I am particularly indebted to my wife, Lauren Rusk, whose editorial magic always works such wonders on my writing style. I would also like to thank my colleagues on the Wellesley faculty, James Finn, Douglas Long, Eleanor Lonske, K. Wojtek Przytula, Randy Shull, and Don Wolitzer for their support. In addition, Steve Berlin, Joe Buhler, Gary Ford, Jennifer Friedman, David Harel, Wayne Harvey, Richard Pattis, and Suzanne Rodday have made important contributions that have dramatically improved the final result.

Contents

The Idea of Recursion

1

Of all ideas I have introduced to children, recursion stands out as the one idea that is particularly able to evoke an excited response.
—Seymour Papert, *Mindstorms*

At its essence, computer science is the study of problems and their solutions. More specifically, computer science is concerned with finding systematic procedures that guarantee a correct solution to a given problem. Such procedures are called **algorithms**.

This book is about a particular class of algorithms, called **recursive algorithms**, that turn out to be quite important in computer science. The use of recursion makes it possible to solve complex problems using programs that are surprisingly concise, easily understood, and algorithmically efficient. For the student seeing this material for the first time, however, recursion appears to be obscure, difficult, and mystical. Unlike problem-solving techniques that have closely related counterparts in everyday life, recursion is an unfamiliar idea and often requires thinking about problems in a new way. This book is designed to provide the conceptual tools necessary to approach problems from this recursive point of view.

Informally, **recursion** is the process of solving a large problem by reducing it to one or more subproblems that are (1) identical in structure to the original problem and (2) somewhat simpler to solve. Once you have made that original subdivision, you use the same decompositional technique to divide each of these subproblems into new ones that are even less complex. Eventually, the subproblems become so simple that you can solve them without further subdivision, and then obtain the complete solution by reassembling the solved components.

1.1 An Illustration of the Recursive Approach

Let's imagine that you have recently accepted the position of funding coordinator for a local election campaign and must raise $1000 from the party faithful. In this age of political action committees and direct-mail appeals, the easiest approach is to find a single donor who will contribute the entire amount. On the other hand, the senior campaign strategists (fearing that doing so might be interpreted as a lack of commitment to democratic values), have insisted that the entire amount be raised in contributions of exactly $1. How would you proceed?

Certainly, one solution to this problem is to go out into the community, find 1000 supporters, and solicit $1 from each. In programming terms, such a solution has the following general structure:

```
void collect1000() {
    for (int i = 0; i < 1000; i++) {
        Collect one dollar from person i.
    }
}
```

Because this code uses an explicit iterative construct—in this case, a `for` loop, though in other contexts it could be a `while`—to express the overall control structure, this strategy is called an **iterative** solution.

Assuming that you could find a thousand people on your own, this solution would be effective, but not easy. The entire process would be considerably less exhausting if you could divide the task into smaller components, which you could then delegate to other volunteers. For example, you might enlist ten people to each raise $100. From the perspective of each volunteer, the new problem has exactly the same form as the original task. The only thing that has changed is the dimension of the problem. Instead of collecting $1000, each volunteer must now collect only $100—presumably a simpler task.

The essence of the recursive approach lies in applying the same decomposition at each stage of the solution. Thus, each volunteer who must collect $100 finds ten people who will raise $10 each. In turn, each of them finds ten others who agree to raise $1. At this point, however, you can adopt a new strategy. Since the campaign can accept $1 contributions, the problem need not be subdivided further into dimes and pennies, and the volunteer at that level can simply contribute the necessary dollar. In the parlance of recursion, $1 represents a **simple case** for the fundraising problem, which means that it can be solved directly without further decomposition.

Solutions that operate this way are often referred to as **divide-and-conquer** strategies, since they depend on splitting a problem into more manageable components. The original problem divides to form several simpler subproblems that in turn branch into a set of simpler ones, and so on, until the simple cases are reached.

If you try to represent this process diagrammatically, you might come up with a picture called a **solution tree** that looks like this:

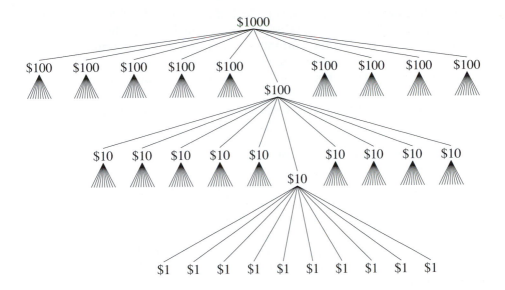

To represent this algorithm in a form more suggestive of a programming language, it is important to notice that there are several different **instances** of a remarkably similar problem. In the specific case shown here, the independent tasks are "collect $1000", "collect $100", "collect $10" and "collect $1", corresponding to the different levels of the hierarchy.

If you tried to translate this strategy into a programming language like Java, you could represent each of these tasks as a separate method. Such an approach, however, would fail to take advantage of the structural similarity of each problem. To exploit that similarity, you must first generalize the problem to the task of collecting, not some specific amount, but an undetermined sum of money, represented by the variable **d**.

The task of collecting **d** dollars can then be broken down into two cases. The first is when **d** is $1, in which case you can simply contribute the money yourself. The second is when **d** is larger than a $1, in which case you need to find ten volunteers and assign each the task of collecting one-tenth the desired total. This structure is illustrated by the following informal method:

```
void collect(int d) {
    if (d == 1) {
        Contribute one dollar directly.
    } else {
        Find 10 people.
        Have each person collect d/10 dollars.
        Return the money to your superior.
    }
}
```

The structure of this program is typical of recursive algorithms represented in a programming language. The first step in a recursive procedure consists of a test to determine whether the current problem represents a simple case. If it does, the procedure implements the corresponding simple solution. If not, the problem is divided into subproblems, each of which is solved by applying the same recursive strategy. Although this book includes many recursive programs of considerable complexity, all of them share this underlying structure.

1.2 Mondrian and Computer Art

During the years of the first world war, the Dutch painter Piet Mondrian developed a new style of abstract art called *neoplasticism,* which is often characterized by rigidly geometrical patterns of horizontal and vertical lines. The tendency in Mondrian's work toward such simple geometrical patterns makes his style especially appropriate for computer simulation. Many of the early attempts to generate "computer art" were based on this style. Consider, for example, the following abstract design:

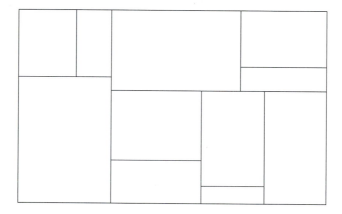

In this example, the design consists of a large rectangle broken up into smaller rectangles by a sequence of horizontal and vertical lines.

For the moment, it is sufficient to outline a general strategy for generating such designs. (The details of the actual program appear in Chapter 9, which includes an exercise based on this example.) To discover such a strategy and determine how recursion is involved, it helps to start at the beginning and follow the development of this kind of design. As with any work of pictorial art (however loosely the term applies in this case), the design starts out as an empty "canvas":

The first step in the process is to divide this canvas into two smaller rectangles with a single vertical line. From the finished drawing, you can see that there is only one line that cuts across the entire canvas. Thus, at some point early in the history of this drawing, it must have looked like this:

But now what? The simplest way to proceed is to consider each of the two new rectangles as an empty canvas, admittedly somewhat smaller in size. Thus, as part of the process of generating a "large" Mondrian drawing, you have reduced the task to that of generating two "medium-sized" drawings, which is presumably simpler.

If you are working alone on the painting, you should at this point choose one of these two subproblems and complete it before returning to the other. Here, for instance, you might choose to work on the left-hand subcanvas first and, when you finish it, turn to the right-hand one. For the moment, however, you can forget about the right-hand part entirely and focus your attention on the left-hand side. Conceptually, the left-hand side represents a new problem of precisely the same form as the original one. The only difference is that your new canvas is smaller.

Once again, you start by dividing your task into two subproblems. Here, since the figure is taller than it is wide, it seems appropriate to divide the canvas horizontally, which might result in the following picture:

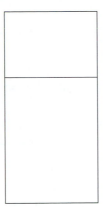

Just as before, you can now concentrate on one of these smaller figures and leave the other for later.

It is important to note that you continue to set aside subproblems for future solution as the process proceeds. Accumulating a list of unfinished tasks is characteristic of recursive processes and requires a certain amount of bookkeeping to ensure that all these tasks do get done at some point in the process. Ordinarily, the programmer need not worry about this bookkeeping explicitly, since it is performed automatically by the program. The details of this process are discussed in Chapter 5 and again in Chapter 11.

As the rectangles become smaller and smaller, you reach a point at which your aesthetic sense indicates that no further subdivision is required. This constitutes the simple case for the algorithm: when a rectangle drops below a certain size, you are finished with that subproblem and must return to take care of any uncompleted work. To do so, you consult your list of unfinished tasks and return to the one you most recently set aside, picking up exactly where you left off. Assuming that your recursive solution operates correctly, you will eventually complete the entire list of unfinished tasks and obtain the final solution.

1.3 Characteristics of Recursive Algorithms

In each of the examples so far, finding simpler subproblems within the context of a larger problem was a reasonably easy task. These problems are naturally suited to the "divide-and-conquer" strategy, which makes recursive solutions particularly appropriate.

In most cases, the decision to use recursion is suggested by the nature of the problem. However, it is important to recognize that "recursiveness" is a property of the *solution* to a problem and not an attribute of the *problem* itself. To be an appropriate candidate for recursive solution, a problem must have three distinct properties:

1. It must be possible to decompose the original problem into simpler instances of the same problem.

2. As the large problem is broken down into successively less complex ones, those subproblems must eventually become so simple that they can be solved without further subdivision.

3. Once each of these simpler subproblems has been solved, it must be possible to combine these solutions to produce a solution to the original problem.

For a problem with these characteristics, the recursive solution proceeds in a reasonably straightforward way. The first step consists of checking to see whether the problem fits into the simple-case category. If it does, you can solve the problem directly. If not, you need to break the entire problem down into new subsidiary problems that have the same form as the original problem. To solve each of these subproblems, all you need to do is apply the same solution strategy recursively. Once you have solved each of these subproblems, you then need to reassemble the individual pieces to complete the solution to the original problem.

Representing this structure in a Java-like form gives rise to the following general structure for recursive programs:

```
void solve(ProblemClass instance) {
    if (instance is simple) {
        Solve instance directly.
    } else {
        Divide instance into new subinstances i₁, i₂, i₃, and so on.
        solve(i₁);
        solve(i₂);
        solve(i₃); ... and so forth for each of the subproblems ...
        Reassemble the subproblem solutions to solve the entire problem.
    }
}
```

1.4 Nonterminating Recursion

In practice, the process of ensuring that a particular decomposition of a problem will eventually result in the appropriate simple cases requires a certain amount of care. If this is not done correctly, recursive processes may get locked into cycles in which the simple cases are never reached. When this situation occurs, a recursive algorithm fails to **terminate,** and a program that is written in this way will continue to run until it exhausts the available resources of the computer.

For example, suppose that, as campaign fundraiser, you decided instead to collect the $1000 using the following strategy:

> Find a single volunteer who will collect $1000.

If you adopted this strategy, and every volunteer you found did the same, the process would continue until the available pool of volunteers was exhausted, even though you had raised no money at all. A more fanciful example of this type of failure is illustrated by the classic children's song "There's a Hole in the Bucket," as shown in Figure 1-1.

1.5 Thinking about Recursion—Two Perspectives

The main advantage of recursion as a solution technique is that it provides a powerful mechanism for managing complexity. No matter how difficult a problem appears, if you can find a way to break that problem down into simpler problems of the same form, you can define a strategy for producing a complete solution. As a programmer, all you need to specify is (1) how to simplify a problem by recursive subdivision, (2) how to solve the simple cases, and (3) how to reassemble the partial solutions.

For someone just learning about recursion, it can be hard to believe that

Figure 1-1. Nonterminating recursion

THERE'S A HOLE IN THE BUCKET
—Traditional

There's a hole in the bucket, dear Liza, dear Liza
There's a hole in the bucket, dear Liza, a hole
Then fix it, dear Henry, dear Henry
Then fix it, dear Henry, dear Henry, fix it
With what shall I fix it, dear Liza, dear Liza
With a straw, dear Henry, dear Henry
But the straw is too long, dear Liza, dear Liza
Then cut it, dear Henry, dear Henry
With what shall I cut it, dear Liza, dear Liza
With a knife, dear Henry, dear Henry
But the knife is too dull, dear Liza, dear Liza
Then sharpen it, dear Henry, dear Henry
With what shall I sharpen it, dear Liza, dear Liza
With a stone, dear Henry, dear Henry
But the stone is too dry, dear Liza, dear Liza
Then wet it, dear Henry, dear Henry
With what shall I wet it, dear Liza, dear Liza
With water, dear Henry, dear Henry
But how shall I fetch it, dear Liza, dear Liza
In a bucket, dear Henry, dear Henry
There's a hole in the bucket, dear Liza, dear Liza
There's a hole in the bucket, dear Liza, a hole

this simple strategy is powerful enough to solve a complex problem. Given a particular problem, it is tempting to insist on seeing the solution in all its gory detail. Unfortunately, doing so has the effect of reintroducing all the complexity that the recursive definition was designed to conceal. If you give in to skepticism, the usual result is that you take a hard problem made simpler through recursion and proceed to make it difficult again. Clearly, this approach is not optimal. What you need to do instead is find a new way to think about recursion.

The difference between the perspective of the programmer with considerable experience in recursion and that of the novice is perhaps best defined in terms of the philosophical contrast between *holism* and *reductionism*. In his Pulitzer prize-winning novel *Gödel, Escher, Bach*, Douglas Hofstadter defines these concepts by means of the following dialogue:

Achilles: I will be glad to indulge both of you, if you will first oblige me, by telling me the meaning of these strange expressions, "holism" and "reductionism."

Crab: Holism is the most natural thing in the world to grasp. It's simply the belief that "the whole is greater than the sum of its parts." No one in his right mind could reject holism.

Anteater: Reductionism is the most natural thing in the world to grasp. It's simply the belief that "a whole can be understood completely if you understand its parts, and the nature of their 'sum.'" No one in her left brain could reject reductionism.

Paradoxically, even though recursion acts as a reductionistic process in the sense that it reduces each problem to a sum of its parts, writing recursive programs tends to require a holistic view of the process. The big picture is what's important, not the details. In developing a "recursive instinct," one must learn to stop analyzing the process after the first decomposition. The rest of the problem will take care of itself; the details tend only to confuse the issue. When one cannot see the forest for the trees, it is of little use to examine the branches, twigs, and leaves.

Beginners, however, often find this holistic perspective difficult to maintain. The temptation to look at each level of the process is strong, particularly when one feels doubtful about the correctness of the algorithm. Overcoming that temptation requires considerable confidence in the general mechanism of recursion, and the novice has little basis for that confidence.

Achieving the necessary confidence often requires the programmer to adopt a strategy called the **recursive leap of faith,** based on the principle that you are allowed to assume that your solution will work for simpler problems when you are trying to solve a complex one. At first, this strategy appears mystical to the point of being suspect. By becoming more familiar with recursion and by understanding its theoretical basis, however, you will discover that such faith is in fact justified.

Even so, it is probably impossible to avoid completely the tendency to undertake a reductionistic analysis. Seeing the details has the effect of justifying the faith required to adopt the more holistic perspective, since one can actually "see it work." Seemingly, recursion is one of those techniques that you must learn, at some level, through your own experience.

Glinda: [To Dorothy] You've always had the power to go back to Kansas.

Scarecrow: Then why didn't you tell her before?

Glinda: Because she wouldn't have believed me. She had to learn it for herself.

—The Wizard of Oz

Exercises

1-1. Given the structure of the "collect *N* dollars" algorithm suggested by the **collect** method on page 3, what would happen if the original target were 500 instead of 1000? How could you fix this problem?

1-2. Using a large sheet of graph paper and a notepad to keep track of your unfinished tasks, follow the steps required to generate a Mondrian-style rectangle such as the one illustrated in the text. Use your own sense of aesthetics to determine where to divide each rectangle and to decide whether or not a rectangle should be divided at all.

1-3. Suppose that there is a pile of sixteen coins on a table, one of which is a counterfeit weighing slightly less than the others. You also have a two-pan balance that allows you to weigh one set of coins against another. Using the principle of divide-and-conquer, how could you determine the counterfeit coin in four weighings? If you solve this problem, see if you can come up with a procedure to find the counterfeit coin in just *three* weighings. The strategy is much the same, but the problem must be subdivided in a different way. Can you generalize this approach so that it works for any set of *N* coins?

Mathematical Preliminaries

One cannot escape the feeling that these mathematical formulae have an independent existence and an intelligence of their own, that they are wiser than we are, wiser even than their discoverers.
—Heinrich Hertz

Many students who have become interested in computer science through their experience with programming respond with a certain level of distrust or disapproval to the idea that computer science requires a strong mathematical foundation. For those students, mathematics and programming often seem to represent antithetical aspects of the science of computing; programming is, after all, usually fun, and mathematics is, to many, quite the opposite.

In many cases, however, understanding the mathematical foundations of computer science can provide practical insights that dramatically affect the programming process. Recursive programming is an important case in point. As discussed in Chapter 1, programmers often find the concept of recursion difficult primarily because they lack faith in its correctness. In the attempt to gain this faith, experience is a critically important factor. For this reason, much of the book consists of programming examples and related exercises that reinforce the skills and tactics required for recursive programming. Another important factor that can increase one's level of confidence in recursion is the ability to prove, through cogent mathematical argument, that a particular recursive algorithm does what it is supposed to do.

This chapter addresses two separate mathematical ideas that arise in any complete discussion of recursion. The first is *mathematical induction*, which is a powerful technique for proving the correctness of certain useful formulae. The second is *computational complexity*, which makes it possible to quantify differences in efficiency among various algorithms. These topics are introduced in the sections that follow. The goal of these sections is not to provide a comprehensive discussion of either topic, but rather to give you enough of a feel for these ideas to aid your understanding of recursion.

2.1 Mathematical Induction

Recursive thinking has a parallel in mathematics that is called **mathematical induction.** With both techniques, one must (1) determine a set of *simple cases* for which the calculation or proof is straightforward, and (2) find an appropriate *rule* that you can apply repeatedly until you have obtained a complete solution. In recursive applications, this process begins with the complex cases, and the rule successively reduces the complexity of the problem until only simple cases remain. Induction works in the opposite direction. You start by proving the simple cases, and then use the inductive rule to derive increasingly complex results.

The nature of an inductive proof is most easily explained in the context of an example. In many mathematical and computer science applications, you need to compute the sum of the integers from 1 up to some maximum value N. You could certainly calculate this number by taking each number in order and adding it to a running total. Unfortunately, calculating the sum of the integers from 1 to 1000 by this method would require 999 additions, which you would quickly tire of performing in longhand. A much easier approach involves using the mathematical formula

$$1 + 2 + 3 + \cdots + N = \frac{N(N+1)}{2}$$

While this formula is certainly more convenient, it will seem appropriate only if you can be convinced of its correctness.

For many formulae of this sort, mathematical induction provides an ideal mechanism for proof. In general, induction is applicable whenever you are trying to prove that some property or formula is true for every positive number N.

The first step in an inductive proof consists of establishing that the formula holds when $N = 1$. This constitutes the **base case** of an inductive proof and is quite easy in this example. Substituting 1 for N in the right-hand side of the formula and simplifying the result is sufficient to establish the base case:

$$\frac{1(1+1)}{2} = \frac{2}{2} = 1$$

The remaining steps in a proof by induction proceed as follows:

1. Assume that the formula is true for some arbitrary number N. This assumption is called the **inductive hypothesis.**
2. Using that hypothesis, establish that the formula holds for the number $N+1$.

Thus, in the current example, the inductive hypothesis consists of making the assumption that

$$1 + 2 + 3 + \cdots + N = \frac{N(N+1)}{2}$$

holds for some unspecified number N. To complete the induction proof, it is necessary to establish that

$$1 + 2 + 3 + \cdots + (N+1) = \frac{(N+1)(N+2)}{2}$$

Look at the left-hand side of the expression. If you fill in the last term represented by the ellipsis (that is, the term immediately prior to $N+1$), you get

$$1 + 2 + 3 + \cdots + N + (N+1)$$

The first N terms in that sum should look somewhat familiar, since they are the same as those on the left-hand side of the inductive hypothesis. The key to inductive proofs is that you are allowed to use the result for N during the derivation of the case for $N+1$. Thus, you can replace the first N terms in the new summation by the formula assumed in the inductive hypothesis. From this point on, it is easy to complete the derivation by simple algebra:

$$\underbrace{1 + 2 + 3 + \cdots + N} + (N+1)$$

$$\frac{N(N+1)}{2} + (N+1)$$

$$= \frac{N^2 + N}{2} + \frac{2N+2}{2}$$

$$= \frac{N^2 + 3N + 2}{2}$$

$$= \frac{(N+1)(N+2)}{2}$$

Even though mathematical induction provides a useful mechanism for proving the correctness of this formula, it does not offer any insight into how such a formula might be derived. Such intuition often finds its roots in a geometrical representation of the problem. In this example, the successive integers can be represented as lines of dots arranged to form a triangle:

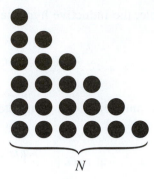

N

Clearly, the sum of the first N integers is simply the number of dots in the triangle. That idea, however, has not simplified the problem but merely changed its form. To determine the number of dots, you need to find an appropriate geometrical insight. If, for example, you take an identical triangle, invert it, and write it above the first triangle, you get a rectangular array of dots that has exactly twice as many dots as in the original triangle:

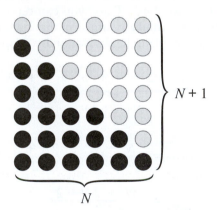

$N + 1$

N

Fortunately, counting the number of dots in a rectangle is a considerably easier task, since the number of dots is simply the number of columns times the number of rows. Since this diagram has N columns and $N+1$ rows, there are $N \times (N+1)$ dots in the rectangle, and therefore

$$\frac{N(N+1)}{2}$$

dots in the original triangle.

As a second example, suppose you want to find a simple formula for computing the sum of the first N odd integers, as follows:

$$1 + 3 + 5 + \cdots + (N^{\text{th}} \text{odd number})$$

The expression "(N^{th} odd number)" is a little cumbersome for mathematical manipulation and can be represented more concisely by the expression $2N-1$, like this:

$$1 + 3 + 5 + \cdots + (2N-1)$$

Once again, you can gain some insight by considering a geometric representation. If you start with a single dot and add three dots to it, you can arrange those three dots to form an L-shape around the original dot, creating a 2 x 2 square. Similarly, if you add five more dots to create a new row and column, you get a 3 x 3 square. Continuing this pattern results in the following figure:

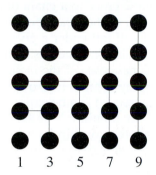

Since you have both an extra row and an extra column, each new L-shaped addition to the figure requires two more dots than the previous one. Given that you started with a single dot, this process corresponds to adding the next odd number each time. Using this insight, the correct formula for the sum of the first N odd numbers is simply

$$1 + 3 + 5 + \cdots + (2N-1) = N^2$$

Although the foregoing geometric argument can be turned into a mathematically rigorous proof, it is simpler to establish the correctness of this formula by induction. One such proof appears in Figure 2-1 at the top of the next page. Both the base case and the inductive derivation are reasonably straightforward. Before turning the page, see if you can develop such a proof on your own.

Figure 2-1. Inductive proof for the sum of odd integers formula

Inductive proof for the formula

$$1 + 3 + 5 + \cdots + (2N - 1) = N^2$$

Base case:

$$1 = 1^2$$

Inductive derivation:

$$\underbrace{1 + 3 + 5 + \cdots + (2N - 1)} + (2N + 1)$$

$$N^2 + 2N + 1$$

$$= (N + 1)^2$$

There are several ways to visualize the process of induction. One is to liken the process of an inductive proof to a chain of dominoes lined up so that when one is knocked over, each of the others follows in sequence. In order to establish that the entire chain will fall under a given set of circumstances, two things are necessary. To start with, someone has to knock over the first domino. This action corresponds to the base case of the inductive argument. In addition, it must be true that, whenever any domino falls over, it will knock over the next domino in the chain. This requirement can be expressed in a more mathematical form by saying that whenever domino N falls, it must successfully upset domino $N+1$. Establishing this relationship between adjacent dominoes in the chain corresponds to using the inductive hypothesis to establish the result for the next value of N.

More formally, it is useful to think of induction not as a single proof, but as an arbitrarily large sequence of proofs of a similar form. For the case $N = 1$, the proof is given explicitly. For larger numbers, the inductive phase of the proof provides a mechanism for constructing a complete proof for any larger value. For example, to prove that a particular formula is true for $N = 5$, you could, in principal, start with the explicit proof for $N = 1$, and then proceed as follows:

> Since it is true for $N = 1$, I can prove it for $N = 2$.
> Since I know it is true for $N = 2$, I can prove it for $N = 3$.
> Since I know it is true for $N = 3$, I can prove it for $N = 4$.
> Since I know it is true for $N = 4$, I can prove it for $N = 5$.

In practice, of course, you are not called upon to demonstrate a complete proof for any value, because the inductive mechanism makes it clear that such a derivation would be possible, no matter how large a value of N you specify.

Recursive algorithms proceed in a very similar way. Suppose that you have a problem based on a numerical value for which you know the answer when $N = 1$. From there, all you need is some mechanism for calculating the result for any value N in terms of the result for $N-1$. Thus, to compute the solution when $N = 5$, you simply invert the process of the inductive derivation:

> To compute the value when $N = 5$, I need the value when $N = 4$.
> To compute the value when $N = 4$, I need the value when $N = 3$.
> To compute the value when $N = 3$, I need the value when $N = 2$.
> To compute the value when $N = 2$, I need the value when $N = 1$.
> I know the value when $N = 1$ and can use it to solve the rest.

Recursion and induction require similar conceptual approaches, each involving a "leap of faith." In writing a recursive program, you assume that the solution procedure will correctly handle any new subproblems that arise, even if you cannot see all the details in that solution. This assumption corresponds to the inductive hypothesis in that you assume that the formula is true for some unspecified number N. If the formula you are trying to prove is not correct, this assumption will be contrary to fact in the general case. Nonetheless, mathematical induction requires you to make that assumption and hold to it until you either complete the proof or establish a contradiction.

To illustrate this principle, let's imagine that you are attempting to prove the rather dubious proposition that "all positive integers are odd." As far as the base case is concerned, everything seems fine; the number 1 is indeed odd. To continue with the proof, you still begin by making the assumption that N is odd, for some unspecified value of N. The proof does not fall apart until you use that assumption in an attempt to prove that $N + 1$ is also odd. Since, by the laws of arithmetic, $N + 1$ is even whenever N is odd, you discover a contradiction to the original assumption.

With both recursion and induction, you have no *a priori* reason to believe in the truth of the initial assumption. If it is valid, then the program or formula will operate correctly through all its levels. However, if there is an error in the recursive decomposition or a flaw in the inductive proof, the entire structure breaks down—the domino chain is broken. Faith in the correctness of something in which you as yet have no reason for confidence is reminiscent of Coleridge's notion of "that willing suspension of disbelief for the moment, that constitutes poetic faith." Such faith is as important to the mathematician and the programmer as it is to the poet.

2.2 Computational Complexity

Many years ago, before the advent of the video arcade and the home computer, computer games were a relatively rare treat to be found at the local science or children's museum. One of the most widely circulated was a simple Guess-the-Number game, played as follows:

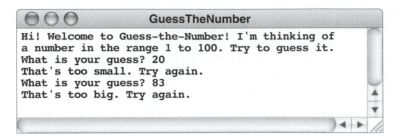

The game continued in this fashion, accepting new guesses, until the player discovered the computer's secret number.

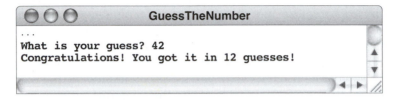

For children who were happy to spend a little extra time with one of these games, twelve guesses hardly seemed excessive. Eventually, however, even relatively young players would discover that they could do better by exploiting a more systematic strategy.

In developing such a strategy, the central idea is that each guess must narrow the range to be searched as quickly as possible, which can be accomplished by choosing the value closest to the middle of the available range. For example, the original problem can be expressed in English as

Guess a number in the range 1 to 100.

If you guess 50 and discover that it is too large, you can reduce the original problem to this somewhat more restricted one:

Guess a number in the range 1 to 49.

This refinement has the effect of reducing the original problem to an identical subproblem in which the number is limited to a more restricted range. Eventually, you must guess the correct number, since the range will get smaller and smaller until only a single possibility remains.

In the language of computer science, this algorithm is called **binary search** and is an example of the recursive divide-and-conquer strategy presented in Chapter 1. For this problem, binary search seems to work reasonably well. On the other hand, it is certainly not the only possible approach. For example, when asked to find a number in the range 1 to 100, you could certainly just ask a series of questions of the form

Is it 1? Is it 2? Is it 3? Is it 4?

and so forth. You are bound to hit the number eventually, after no more than 100 guesses. This algorithm is called **linear search** and is used quite frequently in computer science to find a value in an unordered list.

Intuitively, it seems as if the binary search mechanism is a better approach to the Guess-the-Number game, but it is not immediately clear how much better it might be. In order to have some standard for comparison, you must find some way to measure the efficiency of each algorithm. In computer science, such comparisons are usually expressed in terms of **computational complexity,** which is an approximation of the number of computational steps required to solve a problem as a function of that problem's size.

The idea that computational complexity includes a consideration of problem size should not come as much of a surprise. In general, it seems reasonable to expect that larger problems will require more time to solve than smaller ones. For example, guessing a number in the 1 to 1000 range will presumably take more time than the equivalent problem for the range 1 to 100. But how much more? By expressing efficiency as a relationship between problem size—usually represented by the letter N—and the number of operations required, complexity analysis provides insight into how a change in N affects the required computational time.

As of yet, however, the intuitive conception of complexity is less precise than one might like, because the definition of a "computational step" is by no means clear. For a program that has been prepared for a particular computer system, one approach is to consider each machine-language instruction as a primitive computational step. In this context, counting the number of instructions executed provides a measure of the number of computational steps. Unfortunately, adopting this approach would result in a measure of complexity that varies from machine to machine.

Alternatively, you could try to make do with a less formal definition of a conceptual step by choosing a measure more appropriate to the problem at hand. In the case of the number-guessing problem, the only operation that appears in the solution strategy is that of guessing a number and discovering how that number stands in relation to the value you are trying to discover. For example, you might choose to measure the complexity of the number-guessing problem simply in terms of the number of guesses required.

For many algorithms, the number of operations performed is highly dependent on the data involved and may vary widely from case to case. For example, in the Guess-the-Number game, it is always possible to "get lucky" and select the correct number on the very first guess. On the other hand, one can hardly rely on luck in analyzing algorithmic behavior. Usually, one is more concerned with estimating the behavior in (1) the **average case,** which provides some insight into the typical behavior of the algorithm, and (2) the **worst case,** which provides an upper bound on the required time.

In the case of the linear search algorithm, each of these measures is relatively easy to analyze. In the worst possible case, guessing a number in the range 1 to N might require a full N guesses. In the specific example involving the 1 to 100 range, this would occur if the number were exactly 100. To compute the average case, one must add up the number of guesses required for each possibility, and divide by that total by N. The number 1 is found on the first guess, 2 requires two guesses, and so forth, up to N, which requires N guesses. The sum of these possibilities is then

$$1 + 2 + 3 + \cdots + N = \frac{N(N+1)}{2}$$

Dividing this result by N gives the average number of guesses, which is

$$\frac{N+1}{2}$$

Analyzing binary search takes a little more thought but is still reasonably straightforward. In general, each guess you make reduces the size of the problem by a factor of two. For example, if you guess 50 in the 1 to 100 example and discover that your guess is low, you can immediately eliminate the values in the 1 to 50 range from consideration. Thus, the first guess reduces the number of possibilities to $N/2$, the second to $N/4$, and so on. Although in some instances, you might get lucky and guess the exact value at some point in the process, the worst case requires continuing this process until only one possibility remains. The number of steps required to do so is illustrated by the diagram

$$N \; / \; \underbrace{2 \; / \; 2 \; / \; 2 \; / \; 2 \; / \; 2 \; / \; 2}_{k \text{ times}} = 1$$

where k indicates the number of guesses required. Simplifying this formula yields

$$\frac{N}{2^k} = 1$$

or

$$N = 2^k$$

To obtain an expression for k in terms of the value of N, one must use the mathematical tool of logarithms to turn this equation around, as follows:

$$k = \log_2 N$$

Thus, in the worst case, the number of steps required to guess a number through binary search is the base-2 logarithm of the number of values. In the average case, one can expect to find the correct value one guess sooner, as discussed in exercise 2-5.

In expressing computational complexity, computer scientists often make use of logarithms, which typically arise from an analysis similar to this one in which the divide-and-conquer strategy involves cutting the size in half at each step of the recursion. This process of division by two is what gives rise to the appearance of base-2 logarithms. Following the standard conventions for expressing computational complexity, this text uses "log N" to indicate base-2 logarithms without explicitly writing down the base.

Estimates of computational complexity are most often used to provide insight into the behavior of an algorithm as the size of the problem grows large. Here, for example, the following table uses the worst-case formula to compute the number of guesses required for the two search algorithms:

N	linear search	binary search
10	10	4
100	100	7
1,000	1,000	10
10,000	10,000	14
100,000	100,000	17
1,000,000	1,000,000	20

This table demonstrates conclusively the value of binary search. The difference between the algorithms becomes increasingly pronounced as N takes on larger values. For ten values, binary search will yield the result in no more than four guesses. Linear search requires ten, so the binary search method represents a factor of 2.5 increase in efficiency. For 1,000,000 values, on the other hand, this factor has increased to one of 50,000 — an enormous increase in efficiency.

In the case of the linear- and binary-search algorithms, the mechanics are so simple that it is easy to carry out the necessary computations in a precise form. However, particularly when analyzing specific computer programs, one often has to work with approximations rather than exact values. Fortunately, those approximations turn out to be equally useful in terms of predicting relative performance.

For example, consider the following nested loop structure in Java:

```java
for (int i = 0; i < N; i++) {
    for (int j = 0; j <= i; j++) {
        a[i][j] = 0;
    }
}
```

The effect of this statement, given a two-dimensional array **a**, is to set to zero each element for which the column index **j** is less than or equal to the row index **i**. For now, however, the point is to focus not on the effect of the program but rather on its computational efficiency. In particular, how long would this program take to run, given a specific matrix of size N?

As a first approximation to the running time, you might count the number of times the statement

```
a[i][j] = 0;
```

is executed. On the first cycle of the outer loop, when **i** is equal to 0, the inner loop will be executed only once for **j** = 0. On the second cycle, **j** will run through both the values 0 and 1, contributing two more assignments. On the last cycle, **j** will range through all N values in the 0 to $N-1$ range. Thus, the total number of assignments to element **a[i][j]** for some **i** and **j** is given by the formula

$$1 + 2 + 3 + \cdots + N$$

Fortunately, you have seen this expression before in the discussion of mathematical induction and know that this formula can be simplified to

$$\frac{N(N+1)}{2}$$

which in turn can be expressed in polynomial form like this:

$$\tfrac{1}{2}N^2 + \tfrac{1}{2}N$$

Although this count is accurate in terms of the number of assignments, it offers only a rough approximation of the total execution time since it ignores the other operations that are necessary, for example, controlling the **for** loops.

Such an approximation can nonetheless be quite useful as a tool for predicting how changes in N will affect the total execution time. Once again, it helps to make a table showing the number of assignments performed for various values of N.

N	assignments to a[i][j]
10	55
100	5,050
1,000	500,500
10,000	50,005,000

From this table, it is clear that the number of assignments grows much more quickly than N. Whenever the size of the problem increases by a factor of 10, the number of assignments jumps by a factor of nearly 100.

The table also illustrates another important property of the formula

$$\tfrac{1}{2} N^2 + \tfrac{1}{2} N$$

As N increases, the contribution of the second term in the formula decreases in importance. Since this formula serves only as an approximation, it was a bit silly to write 50,005,000 as the last entry in the table. Certainly, 50,000,000 is close enough for all practical purposes. As long as N is relatively large, the first term will always be much larger than the second. Mathematically, this relationship is often indicated by writing

$$N^2 \gg N$$

The symbol $\gg$ is read as "dominates" and indicates that the term on the right is insignificant compared to the term on the left, whenever the value of N is sufficiently large. In more formal terms, this relationship implies that the ratio of N to N^2 tends to approach 0 as N becomes large—a property that mathematicians express in the following shorthand form:

$$\lim_{N \to \infty} \frac{N}{N^2} = 0$$

Since the practical impact of computational complexity is usually most relevant for large values of N, it makes sense to simplify the formula and say that the nested loop structure runs in a number of steps roughly equal to

$$\tfrac{1}{2} N^2$$

Conventionally, however, computer scientists apply another simplification here. Although it is occasionally useful to have the additional precision provided by the preceding formula, one gains a great deal of insight into the behavior of this algorithm simply by knowing that it requires a number of steps proportional to N^2. This proportionality relationship is sufficient, for example, to predict that if you double N, you should expect a four-fold increase in running time. Similarly, a factor of ten increase in N should increase the overall time by a factor of 100. This growth pattern is reflected in the table and depends only on the N^2 component and not on the less significant terms or the coefficient attached to the dominant term.

In computer science, this proportional form of complexity measure is used so often that it has acquired its own notational form. All of the simplifications that were introduced above can be summarized by writing that the Java statement

```
for (int i = 0; i < N; i++) {
    for (int j = 0; j <= i; j++) {
        a[i][j] = 0;
    }
}
```

has a computational complexity of

$$O(N^2)$$

This notation is read either as "big-O of N squared" or, somewhat more simply, "order N squared."

Formally, saying that a particular algorithm runs in time

$$O(f(N))$$

for some function $f(N)$ means that, as long as N is sufficiently large, the time required to perform that algorithm is never larger than

$$C \times f(N)$$

for some unspecified constant C.

In practice, certain complexity orders tend to arise quite frequently. Figure 2-2 lists several common algorithmic complexity measures. In the table, the last column indicates the name that is conventionally used to refer to algorithms in that class. For example, the linear search algorithm runs, not surprisingly, in linear time. Similarly, the nested **for** loops described in the earlier example represent quadratic complexity.

The most important characteristic of complexity analysis is expressed in the center column in the table. This column indicates how the performance of

Figure 2-2. Common complexity characteristics

Given an algorithm of this complexity	when N doubles, the running time	common name for this complexity class
$O(1)$	does not change	*constant*
$O(\log N)$	increases by a small constant	*logarithmic*
$O(N)$	doubles	*linear*
$O(N \log N)$	slightly more than doubles	$N \log N$
$O(N^2)$	increases by a factor of 4	*quadratic*
$O(N^k)$	increases by a factor of 2^k	*polynomial*
$O(2^N)$	grows very, very fast	*exponential*

the algorithm is affected by a doubling of the problem size. For example, if you doubled the value of N for a quadratic algorithm, the running time would increase by a factor of four. But if you were somehow able to redesign that algorithm to run in time $N \log N$, doubling the size of the input data would have a less drastic effect. The new algorithm would still require more time for the larger problem, but the increase would be only a factor of two over that for the smaller problem, plus some constant amount of time contributed by the logarithmic term. If N grows even larger, this reduction constitutes an enormous savings in time.

In attempting to improve the performance of almost any program, the greatest potential savings come from improving the algorithm so that its complexity bound is reduced. "Tweaking the code" to eliminate a few instructions along the way can only provide a small percentage increase in performance. On the other hand, changing the algorithm offers an unlimited reduction in the running time. For small problems, the time saved may be minor, but the relative saving grows much larger as the size of the problem increases. In many practical settings, algorithmic improvement can reduce the time requirements of a program by factors of hundreds or thousands—clearly an impressive efficiency gain.

Exercises

2-1. Prove, using mathematical induction, that the sum of the first N even integers is given by the formula

$$N^2 + N$$

How might you have predicted this expression using the other formulae developed in this chapter?

2-2. Use mathematical induction to establish that the following formulae are correct:

(a) $1 + 2 + 4 + 8 + \cdots + 2^{N-1} = 2^N - 1$

(b) $1 + 3 + 9 + 27 + \cdots + 3^N = \dfrac{3^{N+1} - 1}{2}$

(c) $1 \times 1 + 2 \times 2 + 3 \times 4 + 4 \times 8 + \cdots + N \times 2^{N-1} = (N-1) 2^N + 1$

2-3. The year: 1777. The setting: General Washington's camp somewhere in the colonies. The Redcoats have been shelling the Revolutionary forces with a large cannon within the British camp. You have been assigned a dangerous reconnaissance mission—to infiltrate the enemy camp and determine the amount of ammunition available for that cannon. Fortunately for you, the British (being relatively neat and orderly) have stacked the cannonballs into a single pyramid-shaped stack. At the top is a single cannonball resting on a square of four cannonballs, which itself rests on a square of nine cannonballs, and so forth. Given your dangerous situation, you only have a chance to count the number of layers before escaping back to your own encampment. Using mathematical induction, prove that, if N is the number of layers, the total number of cannonballs is given by the equation

$$1 + 2 + 4 + 8 + \cdots + 2^{N-1} = 2^N - 1$$

2-4. Assuming that the variable **n** in each of the following program fragments is an integer that defines the problem size, what is the order of complexity for the number of times the loop body is executed (which you may assume takes a constant amount of time independent of the value of **n**)?

(a)
```
for (int i = n; i < n + 1000; i++) {
    ...loop body ...
}
```

(b)
```
for (int i = 0; i < n; i++) {
    for (int j = 0; j < n; j++) {
        ...loop body ...
    }
}
```

(c)
```
for (int i = n; i > 0; i /= 2) {
    ...loop body ...
}
```

If the statements within the loop body take the same amount of time to execute, for what values of **n** will program (a) run more quickly than program (c)?

2-5. [For the mathematically inclined] In trying to locate a number by binary search, it is always possible that you will get lucky and guess the answer much more quickly than you would in the worst possible case. For example, if 50 were in fact the correct number in the 1 to 100 range, binary search would find it on the very first guess. To determine the average-case behavior of binary search, you need to determine the expected value of the number of guesses over the entire possible range. Assuming that there are N numbers in the complete range, you know that only one of them (specifically, the number at the center of the range) will be guessed on the very first try. Two numbers will be guessed in two tries, four numbers in three tries and so forth. Thus, the average number of guesses required is given by the formula

$$\frac{1 \times 1 + 2 \times 2 + 3 \times 4 + 4 \times 8 + \cdots + G \times 2^{G-1}}{N}$$

where G is the maximum number of guesses that might be required, which in this case is simply $\log N$. Using the expression from exercise 2-2(c), simplify this formula. As N grows large, what value does this computation approach?

2-6.   [Adapted from a 1961 essay by Joel Cohen entitled "On the nature of mathematical proofs"] Mathematical induction can have its pitfalls, particularly if one is careless. For example, the following argument appears to be a proof that all horses are the same color. What is wrong here? Is there really no horse of a different color?

Definition: Define a set of horses to be *monochromatic* if all the horses in the set have the same coloration.

Conjecture: Any set of horses is monochromatic.

Technique: Proof by induction on the number of horses in the set.

Base case: Any set of one horse is monochromatic, by definition.

Induction: Assume that any set of N horses is monochromatic. Consider a set of $N+1$ horses. That can be divided into smaller subsets in several ways. For example, consider the division indicated in the diagram

$$\boxed{\text{H}_1 \ \ \text{H}_2 \ \ \text{H}_3 \ \cdots \ \text{H}_N} \quad \boxed{\text{H}_{N+1}}$$
$$\qquad\qquad A \qquad\qquad\qquad\quad A'$$

The subset labeled A in this diagram is a set of N horses and is therefore monochromatic by the inductive hypothesis. You could, however, equally well choose to divide the complete set as follows:

$$\boxed{\text{H}_1} \quad \boxed{\text{H}_2 \ \ \text{H}_3 \ \cdots \ \text{H}_N \ \ \text{H}_{N+1}}$$
$$\quad B' \qquad\qquad\qquad B$$

In this case, the subset B must also be monochromatic. Thus, all the horses in subset A are the same color, as are all the horses in subset B. But H_2 is in both subsets A and B, which implies that both subsets must contain horses of the *same* color.

Recursive Functions

To iterate is human, to recurse divine.

—Anonymous

Chapter 1 defined recursion as a solution technique that operates by reducing a large problem to simpler problems of the same type. That definition, however, does not necessarily imply the use of a computer. This chapter examines how recursion applies in the context of a programming language.

First of all, it is important to remember that the statement of any recursive solution must be general enough that it solves not only the original problem but also any subproblems generated along the way. In the context of a programming language, this requirement usually implies that the method used to represent the algorithm must take parameters that define the specific subproblem. In the case of the fundraising problem from Chapter 1, for example, it is not enough to write a single method to collect $1000 dollars. Instead, the recursive implementation solves the more general problem of raising **d** dollars, where **d** is a parameter whose value will change at different levels of the recursive solution.

Given the need to specify parameters that define a specific instance of the problem, recursive solutions usually take the form of methods whose arguments convey the necessary information. Whenever a recursive method breaks a large problem down into simpler subproblems, it solves those subproblems by *calling the original method* with new arguments, updated to reflect the new subproblem.

This chapter is devoted to a pair of mathematical functions whose recursive character follows directly from their mathematical formulation. For some reason, most students find these functions easier to understand than the more procedurally oriented problems described in subsequent chapters, even though the underlying solution technique is the same. Starting out with these mathematical functions makes it possible to describe the structure of recursive solutions in a context that somehow appears natural before diving into more complex problems whose recursive character is harder to discern.

3.1 Factorials

In word games like Scrabble™, the play consists of rearranging a set of letters to form words. For example, given the seven letters

T   I   R   N   E   G   S

you can construct such words as **RIG**, **SIRE**, **GRINS**, **INSERT**, or **RESTING**. Often, there is a considerable advantage in playing as long a word as possible. In Scrabble, for example, playing all seven tiles in the same turn gets you a bonus of fifty points, which makes **RESTING** or **STINGER** particularly attractive plays.

In Chapter 6, you will learn how to solve the problem of generating all possible arrangements of a set of letters. For the moment, let's look at the following, somewhat simpler question:

> Given a set of seven distinct letters, how many different arrangements would you need to check to discover all possible seven-letter words?

If you think about this problem for a few minutes, you will discover it's not that difficult to solve. In constructing all possible arrangements of seven distinct letters, there are seven possible choices for the starting letter. Once you have chosen the first letter, there are only six ways to choose the next letter in sequence, five ways to choose the third, and so on, until only one letter remains to occupy the last position. Because each of these choices is independent, the total number of orderings is the product of the number of choices at each position. Thus, given seven letters, there are

$$7 \times 6 \times 5 \times 4 \times 3 \times 2 \times 1$$

arrangements, which works out to be 5040.

In mathematical terms, an arrangement of objects in a linear order is called a **permutation.** Given a set of N distinct objects, you can calculate the number of permutations of that set by applying much the same analysis. There are N ways of choosing the first object, $N-1$ for the second, $N-2$ for the third, and so on down to a single way of choosing the last. Thus, the total number of permutations is given by the formula

$$N \times (N-1) \times (N-2) \times \cdots \times 1$$

This number is defined to be the **factorial** of N and is usually written as $N!$ in mathematics.

How would you go about writing a Java function that takes an integer N as its argument and returns $N!$ as its result? The first step is to give the function a suitable name, since the exclamation point syntax used in mathematics is not legal in Java. You might, for example, call the function **fact**. Assuming that this function takes an integer as a parameter and returns the factorial of that integer as its result, the function header line looks like this:

```
int fact(int n)
```

All that remains is to write the code to implement the factorial computation.

To gain some intuition about the behavior of the function **fact**, it helps to look at the first few values of **fact(4)**, including the special case **fact(0)**, which mathematicians define as having the value 1. Thus, the factorials of the first five natural numbers are

$$
\begin{aligned}
\textbf{fact(0)} &=& & & & & & 1 \\
\textbf{fact(1)} &=& & & & 1 &=& 1 \\
\textbf{fact(2)} &=& & & 2 \times 1 &=& 2 \\
\textbf{fact(3)} &=& & 3 \times 2 \times 1 &=& 6 \\
\textbf{fact(4)} &=& 4 \times 3 \times 2 \times 1 &=& 24
\end{aligned}
$$

At this point, you can adopt either of two approaches to solving the problem. The *iterative* approach consists of viewing the factorial computation as a series of multiplications. To calculate **fact(4)**, for example, you start with 1 and multiply it by each of the numbers up to 4. This strategy gives rise to an implementation that looks something like this:

```
int fact(int n) {
   int result = 1;
   for (int i = 1; i <= n; i++) {
      result *= i;
   }
   return result;
}
```

The *recursive* approach leads to a rather different implementation of **fact**. If you examine the list of the first five factorials, you will notice that each line contains exactly the same set of multiplied values as the previous one, with one additional factor. This observation makes it possible to represent the list of factorials in a somewhat simpler form:

$$
\begin{aligned}
\textbf{fact(0)} &= 1 \\
\textbf{fact(1)} &= 1 \times \textbf{fact(0)} \\
\textbf{fact(2)} &= 2 \times \textbf{fact(1)} \\
\textbf{fact(3)} &= 3 \times \textbf{fact(2)} \\
\textbf{fact(4)} &= 4 \times \textbf{fact(3)}
\end{aligned}
$$

or, in more general terms,

$$fact(n) = n \times fact(n-1)$$

This formulation is said to be recursive because it expresses the calculation of each new factorial in terms of the factorial of a smaller integer. To calculate `fact(50)`, you simply take 50 and multiply that by the result of calculating `fact(49)`. Calculating `fact(49)` is accomplished by multiplying 49 by the result of `fact(48)`, and so forth.

As in any recursive problem, a simple case is necessary to ensure that the calculation will terminate at some point. The decision by mathematicians to define 0 as the base of the factorial table suggests the following definition:

$$fact(n) = \begin{cases} 1, \text{if } n \text{ is } 0 \\ n \times fact(n-1), \text{otherwise} \end{cases}$$

In Java, it is easy to take the recursive definition of `fact` and transform it into the necessary recursive implementation:

```
int fact(int n) {
    if (n == 0) {
        return 1;
    } else {
        return n * fact(n - 1);
    }
}
```

The program and the abstract definition have almost exactly the same form. This similarity between the mathematical form and the corresponding implementation adds greatly to the clarity of your program. In particular, to the extent that you are convinced of the correctness of a recursive mathematical formula, the fact that the program looks like the definition makes it much easier to trust the correctness of the program.

With any recursive implementation, you can think about the process of computing factorials from two philosophical perspectives. If you adopt the holistic view, all you need to do is look at the implementation and convince yourself that it corresponds to the mathematical definition. If you insist on adopting a reductionist perspective, however, you need to analyze the implementation at a much more detailed level.

Consider, for example, what happens when a program tries to evaluate `fact(6)` using the recursive implementation of the function. The first step in the process is that the program evaluates the argument **n**, discovers that it is not zero, and proceeds to the **else** clause. At this point, the program needs to compute the expression

```
    n * fact(n-1)
```

and return the result as the value of the function. Given that **n** is 6 in this example, the program ends up returning the result of the following computation:

```
    6 * fact(5)
```

But what is the value of **fact(5)**? Evaluating this piece of the result requires making a recursive call to the **fact** function. At this point, the program "remembers" (by making appropriate notations on a list of unfinished tasks, as described in Chapter 11) that it is in the process of multiplying 6 by the result of a new factorial computation, specifically **fact(5)**. Repeating this process leads to a cascading set of factorial calculations that can be represented diagrammatically as follows:

```
fact(6) = 6 x fact(5)
              5 x fact(4)
                  4 x fact(3)
                      3 x fact(2)
                          2 x fact(1)
                              1 x fact(0)
                                  1
```

When **n** is equal to 0, the cascading computation terminates because it has reached the simple case specified in the **if** statement. Once the computation of **fact(0)** is completed, the program can then return to the previous level of call. By referring back to its list of unfinished tasks, the program discovers that it was in the middle of computing

```
    1 * fact(0)
```

Armed with the new information that **fact(0)** is 1, the program completes the computation at this level and return to the preceding one. From here, it simply climbs back up through the sequence of multiplications, eventually returning 720 as the final answer.

3.2 The Fibonacci Sequence

In his text on computation, *Liber Abbaci,* written in 1202, the Italian mathematician Leonardo Fibonacci includes an exercise that is certainly one of the earliest excursions into the field of population biology. Rendered in more modern terms, the Fibonacci problem has the following form:

> Assume that the reproductive characteristics of rabbits can be defined by the following rules:
>
> 1. Each pair of fertile rabbits produces a new pair of offspring each month.
> 2. Rabbits become fertile in their second month of life.
> 3. Old rabbits never die.
>
> If a single pair of newborn rabbits is introduced at the end of January, how many pairs of rabbits will there be at the end of a year?

To get a sense of the mathematics behind this problem, it helps to trace the population of the rabbit colony during the first few months. At the beginning of the year, prior to the introduction of our initial pair at the end of January, there are no rabbits. At the end of the first month, the only rabbits are the initial pair. Moreover, since they are newborn, February is unproductive, and only the initial pair of rabbits exists at the end of month 2. In March, however, the original pair has become fertile and produces a new pair of rabbits, thereby increasing the colony's population (counting by pairs) to two by the end of month 3. In April, the original pair goes right on producing, but the rabbits born in March are as yet too young. Thus, there are three pairs of rabbits at the end of month 4.

Hereafter, (as rabbits are wont to do), the colony begins to grow rather explosively. In May, both the original pair and the rabbits born in March are in the rabbit-making business, and two new pairs of rabbits are born. Given that there were three pairs before, this results in a total of five. The following table shows the evolution of the rabbit population up to this point:

at the end of month	number of rabbit pairs
0	0
1	1
2	1
3	2
4	3
5	5

Calculating further entries in the table becomes much easier if you notice an important relationship in the data. The rabbits that are part of the population at the end of any month come from two distinct sources. First, since old rabbits never die, all the rabbits present in the preceding month are still around. In addition, every pair of rabbits old enough to reproduce gives birth to a new pair. This number is equivalent to the number of pairs that were alive *two* months ago, since those rabbits must, by this time, be capable of reproduction. This observation gives rise to the following computational rule:

> The number of rabbit pairs at the end of month n is equal to the sum of
>
> (a) The number of pairs at the end of month n-1
> (b) The number of pairs at the end of month n-2

To express this relationship in a functional notation more suitable for Java, we can let let **fib(n)** denote the number of rabbit pairs at the end of month **n**. This notation makes it possible to restate the central mathematical insight about Fibonacci numbers in a more compact form:

> **fib(n) = fib(n-1) + fib(n-2)**

An expression of this type, which defines a particular element of a sequence in terms of earlier elements, is called a **recurrence relation** and is often part of a recursive definition.

The recurrence relation makes it possible to complete the table and answer Fibonacci's question concerning the number of rabbits at the end of the year. Each entry in the right-hand column is simply the sum of the two previous entries, which gives rise to the following table covering the entire first year:

n	fib(n)
0	0
1	1
2	1
3	2
4	3
5	5
6	8
7	13
8	21
9	34
10	55
11	89
12	144

In mathematics, this set of numbers is called the **Fibonacci sequence** and turns up in a surprising number of real-world contexts.

To complete the recursive definition of the Fibonacci sequence, however, it is essential to specify simple cases to ensure that the recursion terminates. In this example, the appropriate strategy is to define each of the first two entries in the table explicitly, since neither of these values can be calculated according to the general rule. Thus, by definition,

$$\texttt{fib(0)} \;=\; \texttt{0}$$

and

$$\texttt{fib(1)} \;=\; \texttt{1}$$

These simple cases make it possible to complete the formal definition as follows:

$$\texttt{fib(n)} \;=\; \begin{cases} \texttt{0}, \text{if } \mathbf{n} \text{ is } 0 \\ \texttt{1}, \text{if } \mathbf{n} \text{ is } 1 \\ \texttt{fib(n-1)} \; + \; \texttt{fib(n-2)}, \text{otherwise} \end{cases}$$

As in the case of the factorial function, you can turn a definition of this sort into a recursive program in an entirely straightforward way, as follows:

```
int fib(int n) {
    if (n == 0) {
        return 0;
    } else if (n == 1) {
        return 1;
    } else {
        return fib(n - 1) + fib(n - 2);
    }
}
```

This solution technique has both advantages and disadvantages. On the positive side, the implementation is correct and concise. More importantly, the correspondence between the implementation and the mathematical definition makes it easy to believe that the program does indeed compute the correct result. Nonetheless, this approach has a serious downside: in terms of computational complexity, the implementation is extremely inefficient.

To understand why this implementation is considerably less efficient than one would like, it helps to examine the complete sequence of computations for a simple value, such as $\mathbf{n} = 4$. The complete computation involves the following recursive decomposition:

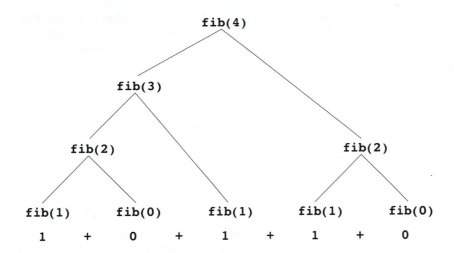

This diagram begins to illustrate the source of the inefficiency. In calculating **fib(4)** by this approach, **fib(2)** and **fib(0)** are each calculated twice, and **fib(1)** is calculated three times. As N increases, the redundancy of computation grows even more pronounced. For example, calculating **fib(5)** not only duplicates the entire set of calculations shown in the diagram, but also requires recalculating from scratch another copy of **fib(3)**.

By counting the number of additions required to calculate **fib(n)** for small values of **n**, it is possible to derive a sense of the algorithmic complexity, as illustrated in the following table:

n	fib(n)	additions required
0	0	0
1	1	0
2	1	1
3	2	2
4	3	4
5	5	7
6	8	12
7	13	20
8	21	33
9	34	54
10	55	88
11	89	143
12	144	232

Clearly, as **n** grows, the number of additions required to compute `fib(n)` by this mechanism grows faster than the result of the process. The entries in the last column of the table suggest that the number of additions required to compute `fib(n)` is given by the expression

$$\texttt{fib(n + 1) - 1}$$

In exercise 3-7, you will have a chance to prove that this formula always holds.

By applying additional mathematics, it is possible to show that the number of additions is roughly proportional to φ^n, where

$$\varphi \approx 1.618034$$

The details of this derivation are largely irrelevant to understanding the computational complexity of the Fibonacci calculation; those details have been left to the mathematically inclined reader as exercise 3-9. The important observation is that this approach to computing the Fibonacci sequence results in an *exponential* algorithm and is, as such, impractical for large values of **n**.

The inefficiency is not inherent in the calculation of the Fibonacci sequence itself, but is instead a property of the solution technique. A much more efficient method of computing the Fibonacci sequence is illustrated by the following iterative implementation of `fib`:

```
int fib(int n) {
    int t1 = 0;
    int t2 = 1;
    for (int i = 0; i < n; i++) {
        int t3 = t1 + t2;
        t1 = t2;
        t2 = t3;
    }
    return t1;
}
```

On the negative side, this program is longer and requires several temporary variables. Moreover, the correspondence between the method definition and the mathematical formulation is not immediately clear. On the other hand, by examining the structure of the **for** loop in the program, it is easy to verify that the program runs in time proportional to the value of **n**. Thus, the new implementation transforms an exponential algorithm into a linear one, which represents a huge improvement in efficiency.

After looking at the Fibonacci example, one is tempted to conclude that recursive strategies are inherently inefficient. Despite the circumstantial evidence from this example, such a conclusion misses the point. The culprit here is not recursion, but the way recursion is used. The recurrence relation

$$\texttt{fib(n) = fib(n-1) + fib(n-2)}$$

is intended only to define the mathematical properties of this sequence, and need not be regarded as an appropriate computational technique. Exercise 3-8 offers you a chance to consider recursive implementations of the Fibonacci function that retain the efficiency of the iterative solution.

Exercises

3-1. Unlike languages designed for scientific computation, Java contains no operator to raise a number to a given power, although it does have a function in the **Math** class that accomplishes the task. Assuming that the exponent **k** is always a nonnegative integer, write a recursive function **power(x, k)** that raises the real value **x** to the **k** power.

3-2. Without using the explicit formula, write a recursive function that computes the answer to the "cannonball" problem from exercise 2-3 on page 27.

3-3. As illustrated in Chapter 2, the sum of the first N odd integers has the value N^2. This observation makes it easy to write a recurrence relation that defines the square of an integer in terms of the square of the previous integer. Write out this recurrence relation, and, by adding an appropriate simple case, complete the definition of the Java function

```
int square(int n)
```

that squares its argument.

3-4. The greatest common divisor of two nonnegative integers x and y is defined to be the largest integer that divides evenly into both. For example, given the numbers 28 and 63, the greatest common divisor is 7. This problem was considered to be of great importance to classical mathematicians, including Euclid, whose *Elements* (book 7, proposition II) contains an elegant solution. The essence of Euclid's discovery is that the greatest common divisor of x and y must always be the same as that of y and r, where r is the remainder of x divided by y. By providing an appropriate simple case, use this relationship to develop a recursive coding of a function **gcd(x, y)** that takes two integers and returns their greatest common divisor.

3-5. As noted in the section on factorials, the number of arrangements of the seven letters in a Scrabble rack can be determined by computing seven factorial. In playing Scrabble, however, one is rarely lucky enough to play all seven tiles at once and must often be content with finding a shorter word. This fact suggests a related question: given a rack of seven distinct letters, how many different arrangements are possible using some smaller number of letters? More generally, this problem consists of determining the number of ways in which one can select an ordered set of k elements from a collection of n distinct objects. Such arrangements are called **permutations.** In Java, the number of permutations might be expressed as the function

```
int p(int n, int k)
```

By following through the analysis in the text, determine the recursive structure for `p(n, k)` and complete the Java implementation of this algorithm.

3-6.   In computing the number of permutations as described in exercise 3-5, the order in which the elements are selected is significant. Thus, "ABC" and "CBA" are different permutations. In some applications, this order is irrelevant. For example, if you are interested in determining how many different sets of four letters can be chosen from the set $\{A, B, C, D, E, F, G\}$, you need to adopt a different strategy than the one used in exercise 3-5. In mathematics, selections made without regard to order are called **combinations.** Although other notations are also used, it is convenient to represent the number of combinations that can be selected from a set of n objects taken k at a time as the function

```
int c(int n, int k)
```

There are many ways to calculate the value of `c(n, k)`. One of the most aesthetically pleasing uses a geometrical form known in ancient China but usually referred to as **Pascal's Triangle** after the French mathematician Blaise Pascal (1623-1662). Pascal's Triangle consists of a triangular arrangement of numbers in which the left and right edges are always 1 and every remaining element is the sum of the two elements above it to the right and left, as follows:

```
                    1
                 1     1
              1     2     1
           1     3     3     1
        1     4     6     4     1
     1     5    10    10     5     1
  1     6    15    20    15     6     1
1     7    21    35    35    21     7     1
1   8   28   56   70   56   28   8   1
```

If you use **n** to specify a row in this triangle and **k** to represent a position within that row, then the entry at position **(n, k)** in Pascal's Triangle corresponds to **c(n, k)**. This numbering scheme is made more explicit by labeling the diagram as shown:

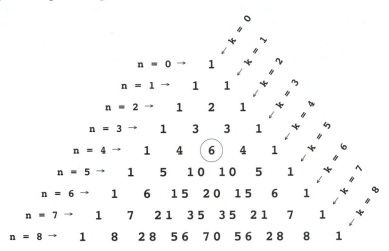

For example, the circled entry at row 4, position 2, shows that **c(4, 2)** has the value 6. In terms of the mathematics of combinations, the interpretation of this result is that there are six different ways to choose an unordered pair from a collection of four objects.

By considering the rule given above for constructing Pascal's Triangle, write a recursive implementation of the function **c(n, k)**.

3-7. Use mathematical induction to prove that the number of additions performed by the recursive implementation of **fib(n)** is given by the expression

$$fib(n + 1) - 1$$

3-8. Consider the following pair of function definitions:

```
int g(int n, int a, int b) {
   if (n == 0) {
      return a;
   } else {
      return g(n - 1, b, a + b);
   }
}

int f(int n) {
   return g(n, 0, 1);
}
```

Compute the values of **f(0)**, **f(1)**, **f(2)**, and so forth, up to **f(5)**. What mathematical function does **f** compute? As a function of **n**, how many additions are performed during this calculation? What is the complexity order of this algorithm? Note that all the work is performed by the recursive function **g**; the function **f** exists only to set the correct initial values of the parameters **a** and **b**. Using a separate method to supply initial parameters is a common recursive programming technique that will reappear in several of the later chapters.

3-9. [For the mathematically inclined] The constant φ introduced in the discussion of the Fibonacci sequence has been known since antiquity and comes up not only in mathematics but also in art. The aesthetic importance of φ is underscored by the names it has been given, which include the *golden ratio* and the *divine proportion*. Mathematically, φ is defined as the number that satisfies the proportionality equation

$$\frac{1}{\varphi} = \frac{\varphi}{\varphi + 1}$$

Cross-multiplication makes it possible to express this proportionality in the form of a quadratic equation, as follows:

$$\varphi^2 - \varphi - 1 = 0$$

You can then use the quadratic formula to find the two solutions to this equation, which are

$$\varphi = \frac{1 + \sqrt{5}}{2} \qquad \text{and} \qquad \hat{\varphi} = \frac{1 - \sqrt{5}}{2}$$

The relationship between the golden ratio and the Fibonacci numbers was demonstrated by the French mathematician Abraham de Moivre (1667-1754), who discovered that the Nth Fibonacci number can be expressed as follows:

$$\frac{\varphi^N - \hat{\varphi}^N}{\sqrt{5}}$$

Use mathematical induction to prove that this formula is correct. To do so, it is necessary to prove that the formula yields the correct values of **fib(0)** and **fib(1)** and then show that

$$\texttt{fib(n) = fib(n-1) + fib(n-2)}$$

for all larger values. In working through the details of the proof, you will find it helpful to keep in mind that both φ and $\hat{\varphi}$ satisfy the equation

$$\varphi^2 = \varphi + 1$$

The Procedural Approach

"Well," said Owl, "the customary procedure in such cases is as follows."
"What does Crustimoney Proseedcake mean?" said Pooh. "For I am a
Bear of Very Little Brain, and long words Bother me."
"It means the Thing to Do."
"As long as it means that, I don't mind," said Pooh humbly.
                          —A. A. Milne, *Winnie-the-Pooh*, 1926

For each of the functions presented in Chapter 3, the necessary recursive
decomposition into simpler instances follows directly from the mathematical
definition. For example, the Fibonacci sequence is most clearly defined by the
recurrence relation

$$\texttt{fib(n) = fib(n-1) + fib(n-2)}$$

Given this definition, the recursive implementation seems the most natural one,
even if it is not the most efficient.

Mathematical formalism, such as the use of recurrence relations, is more
easily applied to the domain of recursive *functions* than to that of recursive
procedures, which is the traditional term used for methods that do not return a
result. Intuitively, functions are mathematical entities, while procedures are
more algorithmic in character. Thus, procedures are less likely to have a simple
mathematical formulation, which makes the necessary recursive decomposition
of the problem somewhat harder to find. Learning to apply recursive techniques
in a procedural context is the essence of thinking recursively and requires a
relatively abstract view of procedures themselves.

To the reductionist, a procedure call is simply a transfer of control that
remembers the address of the instruction making that call. When the operation
of the procedure is complete, control returns to that saved address, allowing the
calling program to continue from the point at which the call was made. From a
more holistic perspective, however, the procedure acts principally as a
mechanism for suppressing irrelevant detail.

For example, many programming applications consist of (1) reading a set
of data, (2) analyzing some aspect of that information, and (3) generating
reports that present the results of the analysis. To the extent that these

components represent independent phases of the total solution, it is helpful to separate them algorithmically by making each component a separate procedure. Adopting this approach leads to a **run** method of the following form:

```
public void run() {
    readData();
    analyzeData();
    printResults();
}
```

The advantage of this programming style is that it enables readers of the program to consider the algorithm at varying levels of detail. At the most general level, for example, you can understand how the principal components fit together by looking at the main program by itself. Beyond that, the individual components of the task can be examined in any order, and only when additional detail is required.

If you think about programming languages from the perspective of human linguistics, writing a procedure has the effect of defining a new imperative verb. Thus, when you write a procedure

```
readData();
```

for example, the word **readData** is added to the command vocabulary and can be used in the same fashion as any other method. Once debugging is complete and you develop the necessary level of confidence in the correctness of **readData**, you can then ignore its internal detail and think of it as a new high-level operation.

In a sense, the definition of a procedure establishes a boundary between two different levels of abstraction. While you are defining a procedure, your principal concern is with the details of its operation. When you call a procedure, however, you are on the opposite side of the fence and need to consider only the effect of that call.

For example, returning to the problem of generating "computer art" outlined in Chapter 1, you might define the procedure **drawMondrianCanvas** (with appropriate arguments to specify the size and location of the canvas) to be the phrase

"Draw a Mondrian-style painting on the indicated canvas."

When you call **drawMondrianCanvas** from the main program, you can ignore the details and accept the English sentence as its abstract definition.

When you write the code for **drawMondrianCanvas**, you need to focus on its internal operation. In doing so, however, you must limit your attention to a single level of detail. As in the case of any recursive program, you need to find a way to decompose **drawMondrianCanvas** into subproblems that have the same form as the original problem. Thus, what you are looking for is a way to divide up the problem into a series of steps that can again be expressed as

"Draw a Mondrian-style painting on the indicated canvas."

for a canvas with smaller dimensions. Fortunately, you already have a procedure that accomplishes this task, and you can simply use a call to `drawMondrianCanvas` with the appropriate set of arguments. And because you are now calling the procedure, it makes sense to think about its effect rather than its internal details.

Admittedly, adopting this conceptual perspective is a bit difficult. Intuitively, most people's minds rebel a bit at the idea of using (especially in such a trusting way) a procedure that they have not yet finished writing. Nonetheless, doing just that is the essential tactical step in writing recursive programs, the "recursive leap of faith." Trying to carry the analysis through additional levels only clouds the picture with irrelevant detail. Metaphorically, looking inside to ensure that the recursive call does the job is very much like Orpheus looking back to make sure that Eurydice is still following—sometimes you just have to believe.

4.1 Numeric Output

To anyone working in the environment of a modern high-level language, the idea of calling a subroutine without first understanding the details of its internal operation should hardly be unfamiliar. In the case of library functions, you to do it all the time. For example, to set **y** to the square root of **x** in Java, you unhesitatingly write

```
y = Math.sqrt(x);
```

because you already have a good sense of what the **sqrt** function in the **Math** class does—it calculates square roots. At the same time, you probably have no clue as to how it does it. There are many possible algorithms for computing square roots. Some implementations may compute a power-series expansion; others might use Newton's method or even reduce the square root problem to its equivalent expression in terms of logarithms and exponentials. In any case, most users have little concern for such details.

As another example, let's suppose that **n** is an integer. To display the decimal representation of **n** in the context of a **ConsoleProgram**, all you need to do in Java is invoke the **print** method, as follows:

```
print(n);
```

In writing Java programs, you have used such statements freely, without worrying about the internal details. In point of fact, this operation is considerably more complicated than it appears.

The reason that printing a number is complicated arises from the fact that most systems are not capable of printing numeric values directly. Instead, any number must first be converted into the appropriate sequence of characters, which can then be transmitted to the output device. For example, if **n** is 1492, the output will consist of the characters **'1'**, **'4'**, **'9'**, and **'2'**, in that order.

To make the problem specification concrete (and simplify it slightly at the same time), imagine that you have been given the following task:

> In Java, write a procedure **printInteger(n)** that takes a nonnegative integer **n** and outputs the decimal representation of **n** using only character output.

Thus, **printInteger(n)** should simulate the function of **print(n)**, but only by printing a single character value at a time.

The complete solution to the problem consists of two largely independent tasks: (1) breaking up a large number into its component digits, and (2) translating each digit into its character code. Since the second is somewhat easier, it is useful to consider it first.

In Java, each value of type **char** is represented internally by a numeric code. For example, the character **'0'** has the numeric value 48. The codes for the digit characters, moreover, are consecutive, so that **'1'** is represented as 49, **'2'** as 50, and so forth. Thus, given a single-digit integer **k**, the corresponding character can be expressed as

$$(char) \ ('0' + k)$$

Now that you know how to translate a digit into the corresponding character, you can proceed to the problem of dividing a number into its component digits. Intuitively, you would like to design a loop structure that would select each digit of the number in turn, convert that digit to a character, and print it. If you follow the discipline of top-down design and leave the details to subroutines, you might start with the following definition.

```
void printInteger(int n) {
    for (int i = 0; i < nDigits(n); i++) {
        print((char)('0' + ithDigit(n, i)));
    }
}
```

This implementation assumes the existence of two methods: an **nDigits(n)** function that returns the number of digits in **n** and an **ithDigit(n, i)** that returns the value of the **i**th digit of **n**, with the digit positions numbered from the left starting at 0. If you write these routines correctly, **printInteger** will operate as advertised.

Unfortunately, neither of these routines is easy to code, particularly if efficiency is of any concern. In fact, after making a few attempts (as described in exercise 4-1), you would probably abandon this course and search for an alternative approach.

To determine whether recursion can be helpful in this case, you must try to find a subdivision of the problem that results in a simpler instance of the same problem. For example, if you can find a way to transform the problem of printing a number into the problem of printing a smaller one, you will be well on the way to a recursive solution.

In searching for a recursive subdivision, it is not enough to find instances of simple subproblems within the context of a larger problem. It is equally important to find some way to reassemble the solutions to those simpler subproblems to generate a complete solution. For example, in writing `printInteger(n)` recursively, it would certainly be legitimate to call `printInteger(n - 1)`. On the other hand, it would hardly be helpful. If **n** has the value 2000, calling `printInteger(n - 1)` would print out 1999. Clearly, displaying 1999 would not accomplish much toward the goal of printing the number 2000.

It would be more useful to find some way to divide a number along digit boundaries so that the solution would consist of printing two strings side by side. The key to finding the appropriate subdivision lies in discovering that it is possible to split a number into its leading digits and its final digit by using the operators **/** and **%**. Given any integer **n**, the expression

$$n \% 10$$

always gives the value of the final digit, irrespective of the size of the original number. The digits that precede the final digit can be determined by the expression

$$n / 10$$

For example, given **n** = 1492, **n / 10** is 149, and **n % 10** is 2. To print out the entire number, all you need to do is write 149 and then write 2, with no intervening spaces.

This decomposition suggests the beginning of a recursive implementation. If you write the outline of the procedure in Java, but leave the internal operations in English, you are left with the following procedure "definition":

```
void printInteger(int n) {
    Print the integer n / 10.
    Print the character corresponding to n % 10.
}
```

This definition does not as yet constitute a complete recursive algorithm, since it provides only the decompositional rule and fails to define a simple case. Fortunately, defining an appropriate simple case is reasonably straightforward here. If a number has only one digit, you can simply convert the number to a character and print it out. Adding this to the informal definition gives rise to the following algorithmic specification:

```
void printInteger(int n) {
    if (n < 10) {
        Print the character corresponding to n.
    } else {
        Print the integer n / 10
        Print the character corresponding to n % 10.
    }
}
```

From this point, all you need to do is replace the English commands with their Java equivalents, as follows:

```
void printInteger(int n) {
    if (n < 10) {
        print((char) ('0' + n));
    } else {
        Print the integer n / 10.
        print((char) ('0' + n % 10));
    }
}
```

Now you are almost finished. All that remains is a single English phrase to be translated into Java:

Print the integer **n / 10**.

Fortunately, you are in the process of designing a procedure that does exactly that. Thus, you have at your disposal a new command that performs this operation, which you can invoke using a recursive call

```
printInteger(n / 10);
```

Thus, the complete definition of **printInteger** looks like this:

```
void printInteger(int n) {
    if (n < 10) {
        print((char) ('0' + n));
    } else {
        printInteger(n / 10);
        print((char) ('0' + n % 10));
    }
}
```

Taking the final step in the preceding derivation does not require cleverness so much as courage. The key to this example lies in a willingness to translate the informal algorithmic statement *print the integer* into a call to the `printInteger` procedure itself.

4.2 Generating a Primer (with apologies to Dick and Jane)

> This is Spot.
> See Spot.
> See Spot run.

For those who attended elementary school in the United States a generation or two ago, sentences like this are almost certainly familiar. For many years, first-graders were taught to read using primer texts designed to develop reading skills through the repetition of simple sentence patterns. Of these primers, the most widely circulated were the *Dick and Jane* readers, in which elementary-school students were introduced to the quintessentially suburban lives of Dick, Jane, and Sally, along with their cat Puff and their dog Spot.

By their very nature, primers use a limited vocabulary and a highly restricted sentence structure. Presumably, this makes them more easily understood by those who are just learning to read. If you look at the *Dick and Jane* style from the opposite perspective, this same simplicity of structure also makes this sort of text easier to write.

Let's imagine that you have been hired to write a program that can automatically produce a reader in the *Dick and Jane* series. As a first step toward solving this problem, you should take advantage of the fact that many of the sentences in the typical *Dick and Jane* story are drawn from a rather simple set of patterns. For example, as the characters are introduced, you usually see a sentence of the form

This is _____   [pattern #1]
       (name)

where the blank space is filled in with the appropriate name.

In addition to pattern #1, there are several other patterns that occur quite frequently in *Dick and Jane*. For example, primers often include sentences of the following forms:

See _____   [pattern #2]
   (name)

or

See _____ _____   [pattern #3]
            (name)   *(verb)*

The last pattern contains two blanks for substitution, and you can fill in each
one independently with a word of the appropriate class. For example, if the
collection of names consists of *Dick, Jane, Sally, Spot,* and *Puff* and the
available verbs are *run, jump,* and *play,* you can create fifteen different
sentences from pattern #3 alone.

 Although it is certainly possible to add more patterns to this list, it is
probably useful to stop at this point and consider the problem of generating
random sentences using the three patterns presented so far. The principles of
top-down design suggest starting at the sentence level, but you can get a better
feeling for the necessary structure if you begin the implementation at a more
basic level. For instance, your first step might be to write a procedure
generateName() that prints out the name of one of the five main characters.
To do so, you could simply choose a random integer in the range 1 to 5 and use
that to select one of the five names.

 Since you will often be making choices of this kind, it is helpful to define
a function **choose(n)** that returns a random integer between 1 and **n**,
inclusive. Such a function is easy to write in Java using the **random** function in
the **Math** class, as follows:

```
int choose(int n) {
    return 1 + (int) (Math.random() * n);
}
```

Once this detail is out of the way, you can easily complete the coding of the
generateName procedure:

```
void generateName() {
    switch (choose(5)) {
        case 1: print("Dick"); break;
        case 2: print("Jane"); break;
        case 3: print("Sally"); break;
        case 4: print("Spot"); break;
        case 5: print("Puff"); break;
    }
}
```

You can use this same technique to generate the verbs:

```
void generateVerb() {
    switch (choose(3)) {
        case 1: print("run"); break;
        case 2: print("jump"); break;
        case 3: print("play"); break;
    }
}
```

In much the same way, you can easily define procedures that generate sentences according to each of the patterns in your current collection:

```
void generatePattern1() {
    print("This is ");
    generateName();
}

void generatePattern2() {
    print("See ");
    generateName();
}

void generatePattern3() {
    print("See ");
    generateName();
    print(" ");
    generateVerb();
}
```

Finally, you can construct a random sentence-generating procedure simply by adding one more level to the structure.

```
void generateSentence() {
    switch (choose(3)) {
        case 1: generatePattern1(); break;
        case 2: generatePattern2(); break;
        case 3: generatePattern3(); break;
    }
    println(".");
}
```

So far, this application depends entirely on procedural decomposition to accomplish its goal. Starting from the sentence level, you first choose a pattern, break that down into its components, and then proceed to select random words as necessary to complete the pattern. At each step in the process, you need to make sure that you consider only a single procedural level at a time. For example, looking at the code

```
void generatePattern3() {
    print("See ");
    generateName();
    print(" ");
    generateVerb();
}
```

tells you everything you need to know about the pattern at this level; the details of choosing a noun and verb are deferred to the appropriate procedures.

As of now, the sentence-generating program is still a bit on the boring side, since it only handles proper names and a few simple verbs. To make things a little more exciting, you can extend the program by adding a new sentence pattern:

$$\underline{\hspace{2cm}}\quad\underline{\hspace{3cm}}\quad\underline{\hspace{3cm}}\qquad\qquad\text{[pattern \#4]}$$

(name)   (transitive verb)   (noun phrase)

The idea is to generate sentences in which the verb has a direct object, such as

> Jane hit the red ball.

or

> Spot found the little green stick.

Conceptually, accomplishing this goal is straightforward. First of all, you need to define a **generatePattern4** procedure and add a corresponding line to **generateSentence** so that **generatePattern4** will be included in the list of available patterns.

```
void generatePattern4() {
    generateName();
    print(" ");
    generateTransitiveVerb();
    print(" ");
    generateNounPhrase();
}
```

For use with this pattern, you can also define a few transitive verbs:

```
void generateTransitiveVerb() {
    switch (choose(4)) {
        case 1: print("watched"); break;
        case 2: print("liked"); break;
        case 3: print("found"); break;
        case 4: print("hit"); break;
    }
}
```

At this point, you are left with the problem of generating a noun phrase. From the sample sentences given above, a noun phrase consists of the word *the,* possibly followed by one or more adjectives, and finally a noun. Just to get all of the preliminaries out of the way, you can define the procedures `generateNoun` and `generateAdjective` to generate words that fit that category in the pattern:

```
void generateNoun() {
    switch (choose(3)) {
        case 1: print("ball"); break;
        case 2: print("stick"); break;
        case 3: print("house"); break;
    }
}

void generateAdjective() {
    switch (choose(4)) {
        case 1: print("big"); break;
        case 2: print("little"); break;
        case 3: print("red"); break;
        case 4: print("green"); break;
    }
}
```

From here, you must finally turn to the problem of the noun phrase itself and determine how the corresponding procedure **generateNounPhrase** might best be defined.

Internally, the structure of a noun phrase is somewhat more complex than the examples considered earlier, since it contains an element (specifically, the adjective) that can be repeated within the pattern. If you think about this repeated operation as a **for** loop, you might come up with the following iterative coding:

```
void generateNounPhrase() {
    print("the ");
    for (int i = choose(3); i > 0; i--) {
        generateAdjective();
        print(" ");
    }
    generateNounPhrase();
}
```

This procedure approximates the desired effect, but there are two important problems. Although you could change the limits in the **for** loop so that the program could produce more than three adjectives, the maximum number of adjectives is always limited by a fixed upper bound. While this may be a useful limitation in the context of a primer text, the corresponding pattern in English allows any number (including zero) of adjectives to modify the noun. The second problem is that **generateNounPhrase** has an entirely different structure from each of the other procedures you have defined, in that it contains

a **for** loop. If you want your program to remain as easy to extend as possible, it
is helpful to maintain a symmetrical structure.

You can easily solve these problems by thinking about the structure of a
noun phrase in a slightly different way. At present, the structure of a noun
phrase can be diagrammed conceptually, as follows:

the _____ _____   [pattern #5]
         (several adjectives)   (noun phrase)

As an alternative, you can define the noun phrase pattern using a two-level
structure. To start with, you can separate out the problem of the word *the* by
defining a noun phrase as having the following pattern:

the _____   [pattern #6]
         (modified noun)

Moving one step further, you can then define a modified noun as
consisting of one of two possibilities: (1) a simple noun, or (2) an adjective
followed by a modified noun. For example, *house* is a legal modified noun
because it conforms to the first possibility. So is *red house*, because *red* is an
adjective and *house* is a modified noun. Similarly, *big red house* is a modified
noun, since it also consists of an adjective and a modified noun.

Since this approach defines a modified noun in terms of other modified
nouns, the definition is itself recursive, and it would not be surprising to see
recursion used in the implementation. In fact, once the definition is out of the
way, the procedures used for a noun phrase are quite straightforward, since they
again correspond closely to the conceptual definition:

```
void generateNounPhrase() {
   print("the ");
   generateModifiedNoun();
}

void generateModifiedNoun() {
   switch (choose(2)) {
      case 1:
         generateNoun();
         break;
      case 2:
         generateAdjective();
         print(" ");
         generateModifiedNoun();
         break;
   }
}
```

In this section, you have learned how to write a relatively powerful primer generator, which can produce the following sentences:

> This is Spot.
> See Spot run.
> Sally watched the ball.
> Jane liked the little house.
> Spot found the big red stick.

These are reasonable sentences. Unfortunately, the program can equally well come up with sentences of less literary merit, like

> Dick watched the little big house.

or even such obvious monstrosities as

> Spot liked the green little red red big red ball.

The problem is that the program considers only the form or *syntax* of its output and takes no account of its content.

The technique used to generate the sentences in this section is based on a linguistic structure called a *context-free grammar*. The name is derived from the fact that, within any pattern, the legal substitutions are not restricted by the surrounding context, even if those substitutions result in meaningless combinations. Although this approach has some obvious drawbacks when used to generate English text, context-free grammars are extremely important to the translation of programming languages and will be covered in detail by more advanced courses.

Exercises

4-1. Without using recursion, complete the iterative coding of **printInteger** by defining the functions **nDigits** and **ithDigit**. In terms of the number of digits in the input number, what is the complexity order of your algorithm?

4-2. As written, **printInteger** does not handle negative numbers. What changes would you need to make in the implementation to correct this deficiency?

4-3. In several of the applications that you will encounter later in this book, you will see that zero often makes a better simple case than one. Some applications, however, can't always take advantage of this insight. In the **printInteger** example from this chapter, the code uses a one-digit number as the simple case. Because printing a number with no digits is even easier, you might be tempted to code **printInteger** as follows:

```
void printInteger(int n) {
   if (n > 0) {
      printInteger(n / 10);
      print((char) ('0' + n % 10));
   }
}
```

This program, however, does not always produce exactly the same output as the version in the text. Describe the difference.

4-4.   Using the recursive decomposition from **printInteger**, write a function **digitSum(n)** that takes an integer and returns the sum of all its digits.

4-5.   The **digital root** of a number is calculated by taking the sum of all the digits in a number and then repeating that process with the resulting sum until only a single digit remains. For example, if you start with 1969, you first add the digits to get 25. Since this number has more than a single digit, you must repeat the operation, obtaining 7 as the final answer. Starting with the **digitSum** function from exercise 4-4, write a function **digitalRoot(n)** that calculates this value.

4-6.   Extend the definition of a noun phrase so that proper names are also acceptable. This change would allow sentences such as

         Sally liked Jane.

or

         Spot found Puff.

4-7.   As written, the most general routine in the Dick and Jane example is the **generateSentence** procedure, which generates a single sentence using a random pattern. Extend the program by adding a **generateParagraph** procedure, which generates a "paragraph" consisting of a random number of sentences. Make sure that the **generateParagraph** procedure operates recursively and uses the same general structure as the other procedures designed for this chapter.

4-8.   Following the general outline of the primer generation example, write a collection of procedures that will generate syntactically correct (albeit meaningless) Java programs. Your program need not incorporate all of Java's structure, but should include many of the more common forms.

The Tower of Hanoi

"Firstly, I would like to move this pile from here to there," he explained, pointing to an enormous mound of fine sand; "but I'm afraid that all I have is this tiny tweezers." And he gave them to Milo, who immediately began transporting one grain at a time.
—Norton Juster, *The Phantom Tollbooth*, 1961

Toward the end of the nineteenth century, a new puzzle appeared in Europe and quickly became quite popular on the continent. In part, its success can be attributed to the legend that accompanied the puzzle, which was recorded in *La Nature* by Henri de Parville (as translated by the mathematical historian W.W.R. Ball).

> In the great temple at Benares beneath the dome which marks the center of the world, rests a brass plate in which are fixed three diamond needles, each a cubit high and as thick as the body of a bee. On one of these needles, at the creation, God placed sixty-four disks of pure gold, the largest disk resting on the brass plate and the others getting smaller and smaller up to the top one. This is the Tower of Brahma. Day and night unceasingly, the priests transfer the disks from one diamond needle to another according to the fixed and immutable laws of Brahma, which require that the priest on duty must not move more than one disk at a time and that he must place this disk on a needle so that there is no smaller disk below it. When all the sixty-four disks shall have been thus transferred from the needle on which at the creation God placed them to one of the other needles, tower, temple and Brahmins alike will crumble into dust, and with a thunderclap the world will vanish.

As is so often the case with legend, this tale has evolved in the telling, even to the point of acquiring a new geographic setting. In more modern times, the Tower of Brahma has become known as the Tower of Hanoi, and it is in this form that it has been passed to today's students as the classic example of procedural recursion.

Before attempting to tackle the complete problem with 64 golden disks (gold prices being what they are), it is useful to consider a simplified version of the puzzle. For example, if there are only six disks, the initial state of the puzzle can be represented with all the disks on needle A:

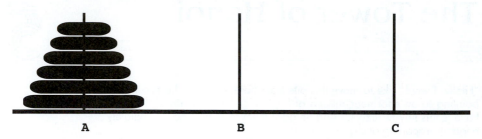

The object is to perform the right sequence of moves so that all the disks end up on needle B:

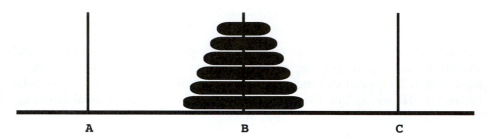

Of course, by the laws of the game (and to avoid ending the universe prematurely), you are not allowed to pick up the whole stack and move it as a unit. You must therefore find some way to break this high-level solution down into a series of individual moves.

5.1 The Recursive Solution

Thinking recursively, the critical point to notice is that the complete goal (in this case, moving the entire stack of six disks from needle A to needle B) can be broken down into the following subgoals:

1. Move the top five disks from A to C:

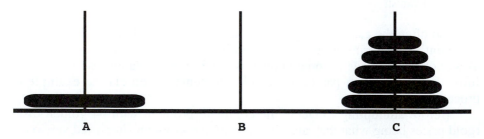

2. Move the bottom disk from A to B:

3. Move the top five disks back from C to B, which results in the desired final state:

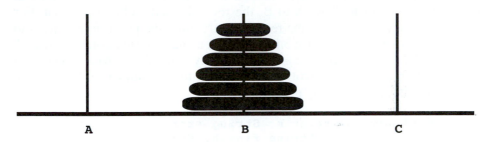

Once again, given the rules of the game, you cannot move the entire set of five disks as a unit. On the other hand, there is certainly no rule that prohibits *thinking* about a five-disk transfer as a single operation, and using that idea as a way of simplifying the problem. Thinking recursively, you know that if you can transform the six-disk problem into one that requires transferring a stack containing only five disks, you are well on the way to a complete solution.

You do, however, need to exercise some caution. In breaking the problem down into a simpler case, you must be certain that the new subproblem has precisely the same form. In the Tower of Hanoi problem, for example, it is important to verify that applying the recursive technique to the tower of five disks does not violate any rules of the game. In particular, you must ensure that a further decomposition of this task will not force you to move a larger disk on top of a smaller one. In the recursive strategy for solving the Tower of Hanoi problem, the rule that larger disks may not be placed on smaller ones is enforced by the structure of the solution. Whenever you move a tower as part of a recursive operation, all the disks in that tower are *smaller* than any of the other disks that might already be on one of the needles. Since they are smaller, you can freely move these disks from one tower to another, even if other disks are already there.

Before you write a program to solve this puzzle, it helps to define the procedures in a relatively informal way. What you need is a procedure that writes out all the moves necessary to transfer a tower of a given size. Since the operation involved is moving a tower, `moveTower` seems like an appropriate name.

In designing a recursive procedure like `moveTower`, it is essential to remember that the procedure is not only responsible for the complete problem as perceived by the outside user, but for a variety of internally generated subproblems as well. Thus, although it is tempting to think of `moveTower` as having only one argument indicating the number of disks, this design strategy will not provide enough information to solve the general case. The statement

```
moveTower(6)
```

tells you the number of disks involved, but offers no insight as to where they start or where they end up. Even though the complete problem is framed in terms of moving disks from A to B, the recursive subproblems are not. For example, somewhere deep in the recursive structure, the program will need to be able to "move a tower of size 3 from C to A using B for temporary storage."

In order to make `moveTower` sufficiently general, the parameters must include which needles are involved, in addition to the number of disks. Thus, `moveTower` has the following procedure header:

```
void moveTower(int n, String start,
               String finish, String temp)
```

where `n` is the number of disks to move, and where `start`, `finish`, and `temp` indicate the role currently assigned to each needle in the current subproblem. Thus, in the main program to solve the six-disk problem, you would expect the call

```
moveTower(6, "A", "B", "C")
```

which can be rendered in English as the sentence "move a tower of size 6 from A to B using C as the temporary needle." Internally, if you reach a position in the algorithm where you need to "move a tower of size 3 from C to A using B for temporary storage," you can express that operation by a call to `moveTower` with the values

```
moveTower(3, "C", "A", "B")
```

The complete solution also requires that you find a simple case that allows the recursion to terminate. Finding the simple case is usually much more straightforward than determining the recursive decomposition, and this is indeed true for the Tower of Hanoi problem. Although you will have a chance to explore another possibility in exercise 5-2, an obvious choice is the case in which there is only a single disk to move. This identification of a simple case leads to a recursive solution with the following form:

If **n** is one, simply move that disk from **start** to **finish**.

If **n** is greater than one, divide the problem into three subgoals:

1. Using this same algorithm, move the top **n-1** disks from **start** to **temp**. In the process of making this transfer, the **finish** needle is used as the new temporary repository.

2. Move the bottom disk from **start** to **finish**.

3. Move the top **n-1** disks back from **temp** to **finish**, using **start** for temporary storage.

Given this informal algorithmic description, you can proceed to the problem of coding it in Java. As in the case of most recursive routines, the procedure definition corresponds quite closely to the algorithmic definition:

```
void moveTower(int n, String start,
               String finish, String temp) {
    if (n == 1) {
        println(start + " -> " + finish);
    } else {
        moveTower(n - 1, start, temp, finish);
        println(start + " -> " + finish);
        moveTower(n - 1, temp, finish, start);
    }
}
```

If this procedure is compiled together with a main program consisting of the single statement

```
moveTower(6, "A", "B", "C")
```

the program will write out a complete history of the moves necessary to solve the six-disk Hanoi problem.

But how? This is the question that often seems to arise when students first encounter the **moveTower** procedure. The recursive decomposition is all well and good as a theoretical idea, but this is a program definition! Where are the details? Where is the solution?

5.2 The Reductionistic View

One of the first things that new programmers learn is that computer programming requires a meticulous attitude with respect to details. When programming is involved, the statements "it's right except for a few details" and "it's wrong" are hard to differentiate experimentally. In a recursive implementation, those details are sometimes difficult to see, because the work consists primarily of keeping track of a list of active subproblems—details that the computer handles automatically.

To understand the underlying process behind that record keeping, it is useful to examine the execution history of a recursive program in complete detail. The Tower of Hanoi problem has two characteristics that make it particularly appropriate for this analysis. The problem is (1) hard enough that the solution is not obvious and (2) simple enough that you can follow the recursive logic without getting lost. With any luck, going through the details will dispel any lingering reductionistic tendencies and give you additional confidence in the recursive approach.

To simplify the basic problem, let's consider the necessary operations when only three disks are involved. In this case, the main program call is

```
moveTower(3, "A", "B", "C")
```

Now all you need to do is keep track of the operation of the program, particularly as it makes new calls to the **moveTower** procedure.

Following the logic of a recursive procedure is often tricky and may not be advisable for the fainthearted. The best way, of course, is to let the computer handle this part of the process, but our purpose in this section is to examine the details. To do so, you must "play computer" and simulate its internal operations. For recursive problems, one of the best ways of keeping track of all the necessary operations is with a stack of 3×5 index cards, recording the details of the current subproblem on a new index card every time a new procedure call is made.

Since you have just made the procedure call

```
moveTower(3, "A", "B", "C")
```

you are ready to create your first index card. On each card, the first thing you do is write down the English interpretation of the call and make that your current goal. In addition, you must also specify the values for each parameter, like this:

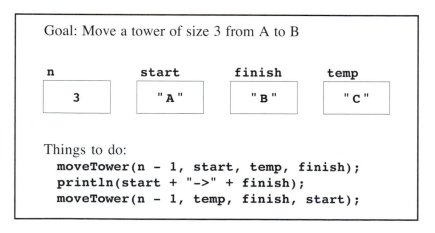

```
Goal: Move a tower of size 3 from A to B

n              start        finish       temp
  3              "A"          "B"          "C"

Things to do:
   moveTower(n - 1, start, temp, finish);
   println(start + "->" + finish);
   moveTower(n - 1, temp, finish, start);
```

On the bottom of the card, you need to make a list of the various tasks that must still be done to solve the problem *at this level*. On this first card, the "things to do" list is simply the statements that form the **else** clause in the **moveTower** procedure.

You can now execute each of the subtasks in turn. Thus, in order to begin the solution at this level, you need to execute the statement

> **moveTower(n-1, start, temp, finish)**

As with any procedure call, the first step is to evaluate the arguments. To do this, you need to find the values of the variables **n**, **start**, **temp**, and **finish**. Whenever you need to find the value of a variable, you must use the value as it is defined *on the current index card*. Thus, the **moveTower** call is equivalent to

> **moveTower(2, "A", "C", "B")**

This operation, however, indicates a recursive call. This means that you must suspend the current operation and repeat the entire process with a new index card. On this new card, you simply copy the parameter values in the order in which they appeared in the procedure call:

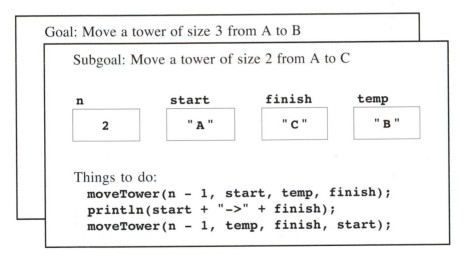

The original index card still has several unfinished tasks, which means you must set it aside until you complete the new subgoal. Thus, in the diagram above, the new card is placed on top of the previous one, hiding the previous values of the variables. As long as this index card is active, **n** will have the value 2, **start** will be **"A"**, **finish** will be **"C"**, and **temp** will be **"B"**. When the operations on the new "things to do" list are complete, you can throw this card away, restoring the original card to the active position. In programming terminology, the information stored on each index card is called an **environment.**

Since you have just made a new call to the **moveTower** routine, you must start over at the beginning of the procedure body. Once again, **n** is not 1, so the first operation is

```
moveTower(n-1, start, temp, finish)
```

In this case, however, the parameters have changed. Substituting the new values (that is, the values on the current index card) into this statement gives

```
moveTower(1, "A", "B", "C")
```

Once again, you have a recursive call, which gives rise to a third level of subgoal:

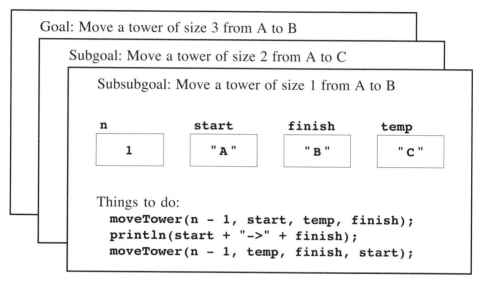

Goal: Move a tower of size 3 from A to B

Subgoal: Move a tower of size 2 from A to C

Subsubgoal: Move a tower of size 1 from A to B

n	start	finish	temp
1	"A"	"B"	"C"

Things to do:
```
moveTower(n - 1, start, temp, finish);
println(start + "->" + finish);
moveTower(n - 1, temp, finish, start);
```

This subgoal, however, represents an easy case. All you need do is write out the string **"A->B"**, and you are finished with the subproblem on this card. Carrying out this operation on the puzzle leads to the following configuration:

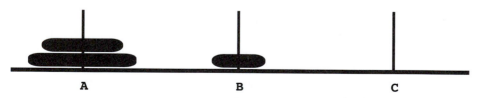

A   B   C

At this point, you are done with the current card and can remove it from the active list. Doing so brings you back to the previous card after having completed the first item on its "to do" list. To indicate that this operation is complete, you simply cross it off and move on to the next item.

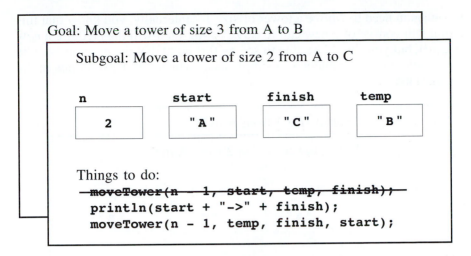

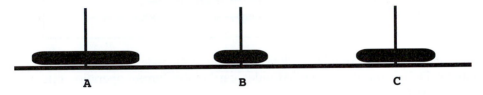

The next operation does not require any further calls; you simply move the indicated disk to reach the following position:

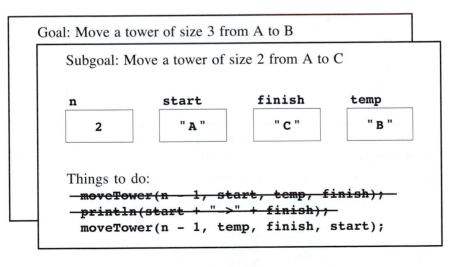

Since you have finished yet another operation on the current card, you can cross it off as well, leaving the current list of pending operations as follows:

Now you again need to "move a tower of size 1." Internally, you know that this operation will consist of a new call to **moveTower** (and will thus require a new index card), but you should be able to see by this point that the program will be able to handle this subproblem as a simple case, which will leave things in the following state:

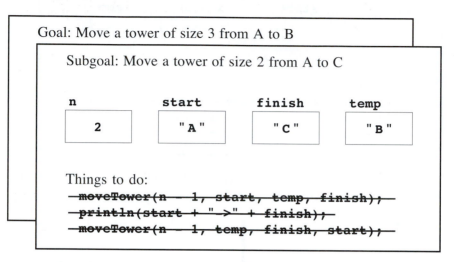

Once again, you are completely done with one of the index cards and can throw it away. Doing so restores the first index card to the current operation pile with the first subtask completed.

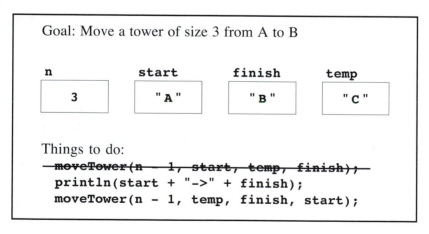

At this point, you have made three moves:

A->B
A->C
B->C

Completing these moves leaves the disks in the following position:

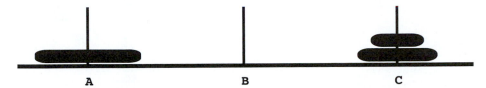

As this diagram illustrates, the program has just completed the first major subgoal and is pretty much halfway through the process. From this position, you need to move the largest disk from A to B and then tackle the remaining subgoal. Again, executing this process will require further decomposition; you should feel free to continue the analysis on your own.

Exercises

5-1. In making a recursive subdivision of a problem, it is extremely important to ensure that any generated subproblems obey exactly the same rules as the original. With this caveat in mind, consider the following decomposition:

> If **n** is one, simply move that disk from **start** to **finish**.
>
> If **n** is greater than one, divide the problem up into three subgoals:
>
> 1. Move the top disk from **start** to **temp**.
> 2. Using a recursive call, move the remaining tower of **n-1** disks from **start** to **finish**.
> 3. Move the top disk back from **temp** to **finish**.

Why does this algorithm fail?

5-2. By following the logic of the **moveTower** function, write a Java function **nHanoiMoves(n)** that returns the number of moves required to solve the Tower of Hanoi puzzle for a tower of size **n**.

5-3. In designing a recursive solution, it is usually wise to make the simple cases as simple as possible. For the Tower of Hanoi program, for example, the best choice may not be that of a single disk as described in the chapter. An even easier case occurs when a tower has no disks at all, in which case there is no work to do. Rewrite the implementation of **moveTower** so that it uses zero rather than one as its simple case.

5-4. Using mathematical induction, prove that the number of moves required to transfer a tower of size **n** by the **moveTower** algorithm is $2^n - 1$.

Completing these moves leaves the disks in the following position:

A little diagram illustrated the problem ...

Exercises

Permutations

The order is rapidly fading
And the first one now will later be last. . . .
 —Bob Dylan, "The Times They Are A-Changin'," 1963

In Chapter 3, you learned how to count the number of permutations in a set. This chapter solves the problem of generating the actual permutations. Solving the more general problem makes use of the same recursive insights but requires thinking about permutations in a more sophisticated way.

Before turning to the problem of generating permutations, it helps to review the basic concept as it appeared in section 3.1, which introduced the term **permutation** to refer to an arrangement of objects in a linear order. If you begin with a collection of N distinct objects, there are N ways to choose the first item in the permutation, N-1 ways to choose the second, and so forth. This means that you can determine the total number of arrangements by computing

$$N \ \times \ (N-1) \ \times \ (N-2) \ \times \ \cdots \ \times \ 1$$

which is simply $N!$.

The goal of this chapter is to write a Java method **listPermutations** that will generate the complete set of permutations for any string of distinct characters. For example, given the string **"ABCD"**, there are 24 (4!) different permutations, as follows:

ABCD	BACD	CABD	DABC
ABDC	BADC	CADB	DACB
ACBD	BCAD	CBAD	DBAC
ACDB	BCDA	CBDA	DBCA
ADBC	BDAC	CDAB	DCAB
ADCB	BDCA	CDBA	DCBA

To display these permutations of **"ABCD"**, you would simply call

```
listPermutations("ABCD");
```

The format of the method call indicates that **listPermutations** takes a single argument (a string) and that it therefore has the method header

```
void listPermutations(String s)
```

The discussion from section 3.1 showing that a set of *N* objects has *N*! permutations also suggests the recursive strategy necessary to generate those arrangements. Starting with the string **"ABCD"**, for example, there are four possible ways to choose the first letter. This observation makes it possible to divide the permutations into four distinct groups:

1. The set of permutations starting with **A**
2. The set of permutations starting with **B**
3. The set of permutations starting with **C**
4. The set of permutations starting with **D**

If you think a bit about these four individual subproblems, you will quickly make an important observation. The set of all permutations starting with the letter **A** consists of the letter **A** added to the front of all permutations of the remaining letters **"BCD"**. Similarly, the set of all permutations starting with **B** can be generated by adding the prefix **B** to the front of all permutations of the remaining letters **"ACD"**. Thus, you can decompose the process of generating all permutations of **"ABCD"** into the following subgoals:

1. List the strings that begin with **"A"** followed by all permutations of **"BCD"**
2. List the strings that begin with **"B"** followed by all permutations of **"ACD"**
3. List the strings that begin with **"C"** followed by all permutations of **"ABD"**
4. List the strings that begin with **"D"** followed by all permutations of **"ABC"**

The seeds of a recursive solution exist in this decomposition because each of the subgoals involves finding all permutations of a string that is shorter than the original. The difficulty, however, is that the subproblem does not have quite the same form as the original. These subgoals all talk about generating a set of permutations and then tacking on some prefix, which was not part of the original problem.

As is often the case in recursive programming, the solution to this dilemma is to generalize the problem. Since the subgoals have the form of listing the strings that start with a particular prefix and then include all permutations of the string consisting of the remaining letters, it makes sense to use that formulation of the problem as the basis for the recursion. The method header therefore needs to include an additional argument specifying the prefix, as follows:

```
void listPermutations(String prefix, String s)
```

The English rendition of the desired effect of this expanded method is

> List the set of all strings that begin with **prefix** followed by all permutations of **s**.

It is easy to recast the original problem to fit this more general form. The set of all permutations of a string **s** is simply the empty prefix followed by all the permutations of the entire string. This observation makes it possible to define the original **listPermutations** method in terms of the new one, as follows:

```
void listPermutations(String s) {
   listPermutations("", s);
}
```

Fortuitously, Java—unlike many languages—makes it possible to define several methods with the same name as long as their parameters are different. It is therefore possible to define both versions of **listPermutations** in the same program. The one-argument method is the one that external callers (usually called **clients** in the terminology of software engineering) use; the two-argument version is the one used internally within the implementation. Thus, if you were including these methods as part of a class that you wanted others to use, you would presumably declare the one-argument method as **public**, while leaving the two-argument method declared as **private**.

Although finding the recursive decomposition is an important step toward solving the general problem, a complete recursive solution also requires you to identify simple cases that allow the recursion to terminate. At first glance, the choice seems obvious: a one-character string has only one permutation. To code the simple case, therefore, all you need to do is write something like this:

```
if (s.length() == 1) {
   println(prefix + s);
} else {
   ...recursive case...
}
```

This code, however, is not quite as simple as it might be. Programmers who are well versed in recursion will be skeptical of using a one-character string as a simple case, since there is an even shorter string—the empty string containing no characters at all—that might serve better. If you adopt this strategy, the simple-case code becomes

```
if (s.length() == 0) {
   println(prefix);
} else {
   ...recursive case ...
}
```

In general, you should always look for the simplest simple case.

The only part of the task that remains is to code the recursive case. In English, the process comes out something like this:

For each character in the string,

1. Remove that character from the string and add it to the prefix.
2. Make a recursive call to list all permutations beginning with the newly expanded prefix followed by all possible combinations of the remaining letters.

This algorithm can easily be translated into Java, as follows:

```
for (int i = 0; i < s.length(); i++) {
   char ch = s.charAt(i);
   String rest = s.substring(0, i)
                 + s.substring(i + 1);
   listPermutations(prefix + ch, rest);
}
```

The complete code for the **listPermutations** method and an associated test program appears in Figure 6-1.

Exercises

6-1. Using the index-card method described in Chapter 5, go through the operation of the **listPermutations** method for the string **"ABCD"**.

6-2. Using mathematical induction, prove the following proposition:

> If the characters in **str** are in alphabetical order (as they are, for example, in the string **"ABCD"**), then **listPermutations(str)** will always generate the permutations in alphabetical order.

6-3. In this chapter (and in the earlier discussion in Chapter 3), the characters in the string were assumed to be distinct. If they are not, the code for **listPermutations** developed in this chapter will generate repeated entries. For example, if you call **listPermutations("ABBC")**, every entry will appear twice. Think about how you could improve the implementation so that the list includes no duplicate entries.

Figure 6-1. Code to test the listPermutations procedure

```
/*
 * File: ListPermutations.java
 * ---------------------------
 * This program lists the permutations of a string.
 */

import acm.program.*;

public class ListPermutations extends ConsoleProgram {

/** Runs the program */
   public void run() {
      while (true) {
         print("Enter a string: ");
         String s = readLine();
         if (s.length() == 0) break;
         listPermutations(s);
      }
   }

/* Method: listPermutations(s) */
/**
 * Lists the permutations of the specified string.
 */
   public void listPermutations(String s) {
      listPermutations("", s);
   }

/* Private method: listPermutations(prefix, s) */
/**
 * Lists all strings formed by starting with prefix
 * and then appending all permutations of s.
 */
   private void listPermutations(String prefix, String s) {
      if (s.length() == 0) {
         println(prefix);
      } else {
         for (int i = 0; i < s.length(); i++) {
            char ch = s.charAt(i);
            String rest = s.substring(0, i)
                        + s.substring(i + 1);
            listPermutations(prefix + ch, rest);
         }
      }
   }
}
```

6-4. Like the problem of generating permutations, the problem of generating all subsets of a set of *N* elements has a simple recursive formulation. For example, if you start with the set {**A**, **B**, **C**}, the set of all subsets can be divided into two groups: (1) those that contain **A** and (2) those that do not. In either case, the subsets in each group simply contain all possible subsets of the remaining elements {**B**, **C**}. Thus, the complete list of subsets of {**A**, **B**, **C**} is

Subsets containing **A**:   {**A**, **B**, **C**}   {**A**, **B**}   {**A**, **C**}   {**A**}
Subsets not containing **A**:   {**B**, **C**}   {**B**}   {**C**}   { }

Using a string of characters to represent a set, write a recursive program that generates all subsets of {**A**, **B**, **C**, **D**}.

6-5. On a standard telephone, each of the digits (except 1 and 0) is associated with three letters as follows:

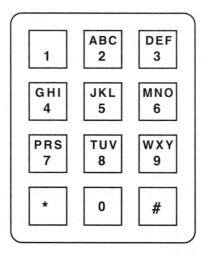

For certain telephone numbers, it is possible to find words that correspond to the necessary digits. For example, at one time it was possible to get the time of day in the Boston area by dialing **"NERVOUS"** (637-8687). Write a program that accepts a string of digits and prints all possible sequences of letters corresponding to that telephone number.

6-6. In the card game Cribbage, one aspect of determining the score comes from computing the number of distinct card combinations whose values add up to 15, with aces counting as 1 and all face cards (jacks, queens, and kings) counting as 10. Consider, for example, the following cards:

There are three different combinations that sum to 15, as follows:

AD + 10S + 4H   AD + 5C + 9C   5C + 10S

As a second example, the cards

contain the following eight different combinations that add up to 15:

5C + 10H   5D + 10H   5H + 10H   5S + 10H
5C + 5D + 5H   5C + 5D + 5S   5C + 5H + 5S   5D + 5H + 5S

Write a function

```
int countFifteens(String[] cards)
```

that takes an array of strings representing a set of cards (using the abbreviated form shown in the earlier examples) and returns the number of different combinations of cards in the array that sum to fifteen. For example, the following code replicates the first example and should display the value 3:

```
String[] hand = { "AD", "5C", "10S", "4H", "9C" };
System.out.println(countFifteens(hand));
```

Sorting

"I weep for you," the Walrus said:
"I deeply sympathize."
With sobs and tears he sorted out
Those of the largest size.
                    —Lewis Carroll, *Through the Looking-Glass,* 1872

In business and commercial applications, programming typically consists of a relatively simple set of operations. For example, report generation is often limited to reading in a file of data and printing it out again in some specific format, possibly including some summary calculations along the way. As long as the operations remain this easy to perform, the fact that these applications also tend to work with vast quantities of data is not an insurmountable concern. Operations such as formatting a report or adding up a column of figures tend to run in linear time. As discussed in Chapter 2, linear time implies that doubling the size of the data merely doubles the amount of time required. For most applications, this increase in running time seems entirely reasonable and well within acceptable bounds.

Unfortunately, not all the operations that characterize business-oriented computing are quite so well behaved. Many applications that work with large amounts of data require the data to be arranged in some sequential ordering. Membership lists and telephone directories, for example, are arranged alphabetically to make each individual entry easier to find. Similarly, bulk mailings are arranged according to ZIP codes to meet the requirements of the U.S. Postal Service. The process of taking an unordered set of data and arranging it in sequence is called **sorting.**

Unlike many other operations that arise frequently in practice, sorting cannot be performed in linear time. When sorting is involved, doubling the number of items to be sorted means that sorting those items will require more than twice as much time. As the size of the data set grows large, the required computation time can explode. To control this phenomenon, it is essential to choose an algorithm that reduces the computational complexity as much as possible.

This chapter considers two distinct algorithms for sorting and compares their behavior. The first, called **selection sort,** operates iteratively by selecting the smallest element on the first cycle of a loop, followed by the second smallest, and so forth. The second method, called **merge sort**, is characterized by the recursive process of (1) dividing an array in half, (2) sorting each piece, and (3) reassembling the sorted subarrays. Conceptually, selection sorting is quite intuitive, while merge sorting seems complex. However, as the number of items to be sorted becomes large, merge sorting turns out to be considerably more efficient.

In describing each of these algorithms, it makes sense to simplify the problem by assuming that the goal is to sort an array of integers. To make the illustrations more concrete, let's imagine further that the specific problem at hand is to sort an integer array named `array` that contains the following eight values:

`array`

90	99	63	82	93	76	81	76
0	1	2	3	4	5	6	7

Your mission, then, is to write a method

```
void sort(int[] array)
```

that rearranges the elements of `array` so that they appear in increasing order.

7.1 Selection Sorting

The selection sort algorithm is characterized by going through the elements of the array repeatedly, selecting the next value in sequence on each pass. On the first pass, the goal is to find the smallest value—in this case 63—which needs to appear in the initial position of the sorted array. Conceptually, one might view this step as removing an element from the original array and copying it to the beginning of a new array, like this:

`array`

90	99		82	93	76	81	76
0	1	2	3	4	5	6	7

`newArray`

63							
0	1	2	3	4	5	6	7

On the next pass, one could identify the smallest remaining value and move it to the next position in **newArray**, as follows:

array

90	99		82	93		81	76
0	1	2	3	4	5	6	7

newArray

63	76						
0	1	2	3	4	5	6	7

Repeating this process until each element has been moved into **newArray** results in a fully sorted array.

This conceptual model, however, is not well suited to implementation, primarily because the operation of removing an element from an array is not easily expressed in most programming languages. For this reason, it is useful to modify the algorithm so that, instead of removing an element, each pass through the array consists instead of exchanging the current element, moving left to right, with the smallest element in the remainder of the array.

To make the operation of the algorithm more concrete, imagine that you are using the index fingers of your left and right hands to mark two positions in the array. Your left hand marks the position that you are seeking to correct. On the first pass, your left hand will mark the initial element in the array, and it will then move rightward one element for each pass through the array. At each pass, you scan across the array from the left hand pointer to the end and mark the smallest value with your right hand. Thus, the positions of your hands at the end of the first pass through the array are

array

90	99	63	82	93	76	81	76
0	1	2	3	4	5	6	7
lh		rh					

If you then exchange the elements in the cells to which your fingers are pointing, the array will be left in the following order:

array

63	99	90	82	93	76	81	76
0	1	2	3	4	5	6	7
lh		rh					

At this point, the element at index position 0 is correctly in place, and the items yet to be sorted are in positions 1 through 7. If you repeat this operation for each remaining position, you will end up with all the elements in order.

Translating this algorithm into Java is quite straightforward, particularly if you apply the principles of top-down design. The essence of the algorithm is represented by the following method:

```java
void sort(int[] array) {
    for (int lh = 0; lh < array.length - 1; lh++) {
        int rh = findSmallest(array, lh);
        swapElements(array, lh, rh);
    }
}
```

The remaining procedures are equally easy to code and appear in full in Figure 7-1.

The selection sort algorithm in Figure 7-1 is effective in the sense that it correctly sorts the array, but turns out to be extremely inefficient, particularly for larger arrays. To assess its efficiency quantitatively, however, it is necessary to choose a basis for comparison that will make it possible to evaluate selection sort with respect to other sorting algorithms. Although many characteristics of program operation are important in practice (such as how much memory the algorithm uses or how well it operates on arrays that are already partially ordered), one of the most useful metrics is the computational complexity of the algorithm, as discussed in Chapter 2.

To assess the computational complexity of an algorithm of this sort, the most common strategy is to choose some operation in the program and count the number of times it is performed. To ensure that this measure is at all useful, however, it is important to select an operation that occurs as often as any other, typically from the innermost loop. In the code for selection sort shown in Figure 7-1, the innermost loop is the one in **findSmallest**, which is executed once for each cycle of the loop in **sort**. Looking at that code makes it clear that the most frequently executed operation in the program is the comparison in the **if** statement

```java
if (array[i] < array[rh])
```

A useful measure of computational complexity, therefore, is how many of these comparisons are performed as a function of the size of the array.

Using the eight-element example presented earlier, it is easy to count the number of comparisons required for each cycle of the **sort** program. On the first cycle, **findSmallest** is called with **start** equal to 0, which requires seven comparisons—one for each cycle of the loop

```java
for (int i = start + 1; i < array.length; i++) {
```

Figure 7-1. Code for the selection sort algorithm

```
/* Method: sort(array) */
/**
 * Sorts an array of integers into ascending order.
 */
   public void sort(int[] array) {
       for (int lh = 0; lh < array.length - 1; lh++) {
           int rh = findSmallest(array, lh);
           swapElements(array, lh, rh);
       }
   }

/* Private method: findSmallest(array, start) */
/**
 * Finds the smallest element in the array between the
 * specified start position and the end of the array and
 * returns the index of that element.
 */
   private int findSmallest(int[] array, int start) {
       int rh = start;
       for (int i = start + 1; i < array.length; i++) {
           if (array[i] < array[rh]) {
               rh = i;
           }
       }
       return rh;
   }

/* Private method: swapElements(array, p1, p2) */
/**
 * Exchanges the array elements at index positions p1
 * and p2.
 */
   private void swapElements(int[] array, int p1, int p2) {
       int tmp = array[p1];
       array[p1] = array[p2];
       array[p2] = tmp;
   }
```

On the second cycle of **sort**, there are six comparisons, five on the third, and so on. Thus, the total number of comparisons in the eight-element example is

$$7 + 6 + 5 + 4 + 3 + 2 + 1 \quad = \quad 28$$

More generally, if the original array contains N elements, the number of comparisons is

$$(N-1) + (N-2) + \cdots + 3 + 2 + 1$$

If you take advantage of the formula for the sum of the first N numbers from Chapter 2, you can simplify the result to

$$\frac{(N-1)\,N}{2}$$

which looks like this in polynomial form:

$$\tfrac{1}{2} N^2 - \tfrac{1}{2} N$$

You can now apply the simplification rules from Chapter 2 to obtain the complexity order. The second term in the formula becomes insignificant for large values of N, so it is appropriate to ignore it in the qualitative expression of complexity. Similarly, the constant factor of $\frac{1}{2}$ adds no insight to the way the time required for selection sort increases as a function of N. Thus, the conventional way to express the complexity of selection sort is simply

$$O(N^2)$$

The derivation of this result is almost exactly the same as that of the nested loop example presented in Chapter 2. In particular, the computational characteristics are just as inefficient. The dimensions of the problem are indicated by the following table:

N	number of comparisons
10	45
20	190
50	1,225
100	4,950
1,000	499,500
10,000	49,995,000

From this table, it is easy to see that the number of comparisons required grows much more quickly than the number of items to be sorted. For small values of N, this fact is not particularly significant. As N gets larger, however, the cost of selection sort soon becomes a matter of concern. For example, if the computer you were using could perform 10,000,000 comparisons per second, sorting 10,000 data items by this method would take about five seconds. Although this time is short on a human scale, it nonetheless represents a huge number of operations. To sort 100,000 items, the program would require nearly 5,000,000,000 comparisons, which would take a little more than eight minutes. And sorting a million items would require 500 billion comparisons, which would take almost 14 hours at the same rate of computation.

As these figures indicate, such algorithmic inefficiency makes selection sorting unacceptable for applications involving large collections of data. Fortunately, it is possible to do better by adopting a recursive approach.

7.2 Merge Sorting

The first step in looking for a recursive solution to the sorting problem is discovering what characteristics of sorting might make it appropriate for recursive strategies. To do so, it helps to review the conditions required for applying a recursive technique:

1. There must be some way to break large problems down into simpler instances of the same problem.

2. Assuming that each of those subproblems can be solved by successive applications of the recursive procedure, there must be some way to generate a solution to the original problem from the solution to each of the smaller parts.

3. It must be possible to identify a set of simple cases that can be solved directly, without any further decomposition.

How well do these conditions apply to sorting?

In seeking a recursive solution, it often helps to identify the simple cases first. Given that the problem is sorting an array of size N, the easiest cases are when $N = 1$, or even easier, when $N = 0$. In either case—an array with a single element or one with no elements—the array must already be sorted. Thus, in a recursive algorithm for sorting, the simple cases require no work at all.

Now that the simple cases are out of the way, it is appropriate to return to the more complicated task of finding a recursive subdivision. You can break up a large array into smaller ones in a variety of different ways. In seeking to reduce the computational complexity of an algorithm, however, it often helps to divide the problem into subproblems that are approximately equal in size. In general, doing so takes maximum advantage of the divide-and-conquer strategy and ensures that the size of the resulting subproblems diminishes quickly as the recursive solution proceeds. Thus, in this case, the most promising approach is to (1) divide the array in half, (2) sort each of the subarrays using a recursive call, and (3) find some way to reassemble the two subarrays into a fully sorted array.

Even though you have yet to specify the details of these individual steps, it is nonetheless possible to sketch the structure of the implementation in **pseudocode,** which consists of bits of code in some programming language intermixed with English descriptions of any missing parts. In this example, the pseudocode version of the code looks like this:

```
void sort(int[] array) {
    if (there is any work to do) {
        Divide the array in half, creating two subarrays called a1 and a2.
        Recursively sort subarray a1.
        Recursively sort subarray a2.
        Reassemble the two sorted subarrays into the original array.
    }
}
```

The test for the simple case is easy enough to code. Since an array with no elements or just a single element is already sorted, there is work to do only if the number of elements in the array is greater than 1. Thus, the **if** statement in the first line looks like this:

```
if (array.length > 1) {
```

The next step is to begin translating the pseudocode for the body of the program. The first step in the English expression of the algorithm is

Divide the array in half, creating two subarrays called **a1** *and* **a2**.

This step would be easy if there were a **subarray** method for arrays similar to the **substring** method available for strings; in fact, since such a method would be so useful, it is worth writing one as part of the solution. The following method creates a new subarray from an existing array and two integers marking positions in the array:

```
int[] subarray(int[] array, int p1, int p2) {
    int[] result = new int[p2 - p1];
    for (int i = p1; i < p2; i++) {
        result[i - p1] = array[i];
    }
    return result;
}
```

The subarray created by this method consists of the elements from the original array starting at **p1** and continuing up to but not including **p2**, which makes the interpretation of the arguments consistent with **substring**. Defining this method makes it simple to create the two subarrays, as follows:

```
int half = array.length / 2;
int[] a1 = subarray(array, 0, half);
int[] a2 = subarray(array, half, array.length);
```

The next two lines of the pseudocode solution consist of sorting each of the subarrays recursively. That's easy. The recursive leap of faith suggests that the recursive calls to the original **sort** method will work as long as the arguments to **sort** specify a simpler case. Thus, the next two lines are simply

```
sort(a1);
sort(a2);
```

But where do you go from here? At this point, you have two subarrays that are each sorted, as follows:

a1

63	82	90	99
0	1	2	3

a2

76	76	81	93
0	1	2	3

How can you reconstruct a sorted version of the original array from these two sorted pieces?

If you think about it, you will realize that the problem of merging two sorted arrays into a larger array is considerably simpler than the more general sorting problem. The increase in efficiency comes from the fact that, in order to choose the next element for the combined array, you need to look at only one element from each subarray. At each step in the process, the next element in the combined array will be first unused value in one of the subarrays, whichever is smallest.

The merge operation is sufficiently complicated that it makes sense to write it as a separate method. The last line of the **sort** method can therefore be a call to the method

```
void merge(int[] array, int[] a1, int[] a2)
```

which takes two sorted subarrays, **a1** and **a2**, and merges them back into **array**, which must be large enough to accommodate both pieces. To keep track of the current position in each subarray, it makes sense to introduce index variables **i1** and **i2** and initialize them so that they indicate the beginning of each subarray, as follows:

a1

63	82	90	99
0	1	2	3

☞
i1

a2

76	76	81	93
0	1	2	3

☞
i2

The general procedure for performing the merge operation consists of (1) choosing the smaller of the elements at positions **i1** and **i2**, (2) copying that element into the next position in the original array, and (3) incrementing either **i1** or **i2**, depending on which element you selected.

On the first cycle, 63 is less than 76, so you choose the first data value from position **i1**. You copy this value into the first element in **array** and then increment **i1** to point to the next element in the first subarray. Executing this step gives rise to the following situation:

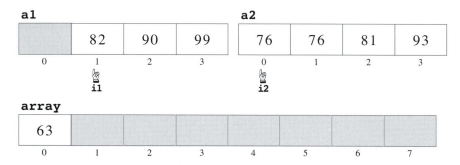

For each of the next three cycles, the value to be chosen comes from the second subarray, so the **i2** position index will move up to 3 as the elements in positions 0 through 2 are copied into **array**, which results in the following configuration:

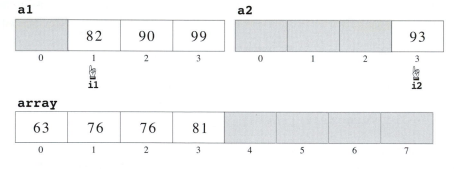

When the remaining elements have been processed in the same way, **array** will contain the completely sorted array.

array

63	76	76	81	82	90	93	99
0	1	2	3	4	5	6	7

Conceptually, the **merge** method has the following pseudocode form:

```
void merge(int[] array, int[] a1, int[] a2) {
    int i1 = 0;
    int i2 = 0;
    for (int i = 0; i < array.length; i++) {
        if (the element from a1 should be chosen before a2) {
            array[i] = a1[i1];
            i1++;
        } else {
            array[i] = a2[i2];
            i2++;
        }
    }
}
```

Of course, the implementation is not complete until you replace the English phrase

> *the element from* **a1** *should be chosen before* **a2**

with a Java conditional expression that has the desired effect. In the usual case, the condition that belongs in this position is simply

```
a1[i1] < a2[i2]
```

but this expression doesn't cover all the possible cases. At some point, the elements in one of the subarrays will be exhausted, and the remaining elements will have to come from the other. Thus, it is necessary to consider whether any elements remain in each of the subarrays before making the comparison. The next element should come from the first subarray if

1. There are no more elements in the second subarray, or
2. There are additional elements in the first subarray, and the next element in **a1** is in fact smaller than **a2**.

You can tell whether there are more elements in a subarray by checking to see whether the index for that subarray is less than its length. Thus, the conditional expression that determines whether to choose the first subarray is

```
i2 == n2 || (i1 < n1 && a1[i1] < a2[i2])
```

where the variables **n1** and **n2** represent the lengths of the two subarrays. That insight is all you need to complete the code for the merge sort algorithm, which appears in full in Figure 7-2.

The code in Figure 7-2 offers a working implementation of the merge sort algorithm, but there is as yet no evidence that it provides any increase in performance over selection sorting. To compare the performance of the two algorithms, it is important to analyze the computational complexity of merge sort.

To begin analyzing the operation of merge sort, it helps to draw a diagram of the recursive decomposition:

Sorting an array of size 8

requires

Merging two arrays of size 4

which requires

Merging four arrays of size 2

which requires

Merging eight arrays of size 1

At each level, all the real work is done by the **merge** method, which runs in linear time in proportion to the size of its sublists. Moreover, at each successive level of the diagram, there are twice as many sublists, each of which is half as large as the lists at the preceding level. Given that the **merge** operation is linear with respect to the number of elements to be merged, dividing the size of the list in half cuts the time requirements in half. However, since there are twice as many **merge** operations to perform, the work required at each level remains constant. Thus, the total work is proportional to the cost of the **merge** operation for the first level multiplied by the number of levels.

The number of levels in the decomposition is simply the number of times it is possible to divide the original array in half before the size of the resulting subarrays reaches 1. As in the discussion of the Guess-the-Number game in Chapter 2, that number is given by the base-2 logarithm of the number of elements. Thus, in the general case, there are log N levels of recursive call, each of which requires linear time. Thus, the computational complexity of the algorithm as a whole is

$$O(N \log N)$$

Unless you have some experience with computational complexity, it may not be immediately clear from looking at this formula that merge sort will run considerably more efficiently than selection sort. To show that merge sort

Figure 7-2. Code for the merge sort algorithm

```
/* Method: sort(array) */
/**
 * Sorts an array of integers into ascending order.
 */
   public void sort(int[] array) {
       if (array.length > 1) {
           int half = array.length / 2;
           int[] a1 = subarray(array, 0, half);
           int[] a2 = subarray(array, half, array.length);
           sort(a1);
           sort(a2);
           merge(array, a1, a2);
       }
   }
/* Method: merge(array, a1, a2) */
/**
 * Merges the sorted subarrays a1 and a2 into array.
 */
   private void merge(int[] array, int[] a1, int[] a2) {
       int n1 = a1.length;
       int n2 = a2.length;
       int i1 = 0;
       int i2 = 0;
       for (int i = 0; i < array.length; i++) {
           if (i2 == n2 || (i1 < n1 && a1[i1] < a2[i2])) {
               array[i] = a1[i1];
               i1++;
           } else {
               array[i] = a2[i2];
               i2++;
           }
       }
   }
/* Method: subarray(array, p1, p2) */
/**
 * Returns a subarray consisting of the elements of array
 * starting at p1 up to but not including p2.
 */
   private int[] subarray(int[] array, int p1, int p2) {
       int[] result = new int[p2 - p1];
       for (int i = p1; i < p2; i++) {
           result[i - p1] = array[i];
       }
       return result;
   }
```

indeeed represents an enormous improvement, it helps to make a table comparing the N^2 behavior of selection sort with that of the $N \log N$ performance of merge sort:

N	N^2	N log N
10	100	33
20	400	86
50	2,500	282
100	10,000	664
1,000	1,000,000	9,966
10,000	100,000,000	132,877

From the table, it appears as if the computational behavior of merge sort is dramatically better than that of selection sort, but it is important to keep in mind that the computational complexity calculations involved in big-O notation invariably ignore much of the underlying detail. In particular, big-O notation throws away the coefficient in front of the leading term. From the complete analysis of selection sort, the actual number of comparison operations was

$$\tfrac{1}{2} N^2 - \tfrac{1}{2} N$$

which means that the figures in the center column are too high by at least a factor of two. Similarly, the figures in the last column are probably too low. The merge sort algorithm requires a fair amount of additional work beyond that required for selection sort, such as the allocation of the subarrays. Thus, although the qualitative performance of the merge sort algorithm is $O(N \log N)$, the constant term indicating the cost of each individual cycle is likely to be much larger. At a guess, you might discover, for example, that the extra bookkeeping work required by merge sort means that the actual running time, relative to the standard set by selection sort, is more accurately represented as five times the $N \log N$ estimate. In that case, a more accurate comparison table would look like this:

N	$\tfrac{1}{2}N^2$	5N log N
10	50	166
20	200	432
50	1,250	1,411
100	5,000	3,322
1,000	500,000	49,829
10,000	50,000,000	646,385

Figure 7-3. Measured running times of the sort algorithms

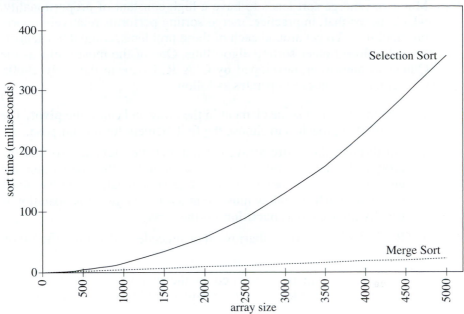

This table leads to a more interesting conclusion. As long as N is reasonably small, merge sorting takes more time than selection sorting. As soon as N gets larger than about 60, however, merge sorting begins to pull into the lead. The bottom line remains impressive. To sort 10,000 items using merge sorting requires only 1.3% of the time that selection sorting would require—a savings of 98.7%. This savings for large arrays is illustrated more dramatically by Figure 7-3, which graphs the measured running times of the two algorithms on arrays of varying sizes.

Exercises

7-1. Deal a hand of thirteen playing cards and sort it using the merge sort procedure described in the text. Use this experience to defend the notion that, even though merge sorting may be computationally superior, selection sorting still has its place.

7-2. Recode the selection sort algorithm from Figure 7-1 so that it operates recursively.

7-3. Even though merge sorting is computationally more efficient than many of its competitors, it has its problems. First of all, since the **merge** procedure allocates two temporary subarrays, the algorithm requires

twice as much storage as an algorithm that sorts the array "in place."
Moreover, merge sort tends to have a high constant of proportionality,
which means that, in practice, merge sorting performs relatively poorly
on small lists. To get around each of these problems, computer scientists
have developed other sorting algorithms. One of the most useful is the
Quicksort algorithm, developed by C. A. R. Hoare in the early 1960s.
Conceptually, Quicksort operates as follows:

1. Arbitrarily select some element in the array and call it the **pivot.** The
    simplest approach is to choose the first element for this purpose.

2. Go through the entire array, rearranging the elements so that the
    array is divided into two subarrays separated by the pivot value. All
    elements that come before the pivot must be smaller than the pivot,
    while those which follow must be at least as large. This operation is
    usually referred to as **partitioning** the array.

3. Recursively sort the subarrays that precede and follow the pivot,
    respectively.

This process can be illustrated in the context of the array used
throughout the examples from this chapter. Initially, the array contains
the elements

array

90	99	63	82	93	76	81	76
0	1	2	3	4	5	6	7

If you choose the first element as the pivot, the goal of the partitioning
step is to divide the elements into those that are smaller than the pivot
and those that are at least as large. At the end of the partition step, the
elements in the array should be reordered so that the pivot element
comes between a set of smaller elements to its left and a set of larger
ones to its right, as follows:

array

76	63	82	76	81	90	99	93
0	1	2	3	4	5	6	7

P

Once you have completed the partition step, sorting the subarrays before
and after the pivot results in a completely sorted list.

It is important to note that the actual array you get after the
partitioning step depends entirely on how you implement the partition
operation. The only requirement for partition is that the the elements

before and after the pivot value in the partitioned list are correctly oriented with respect to the pivot. There are no requirements as to how they get there or how they are oriented with respect to each other.

Given this flexibility, there are many acceptable methods for accomplishing the partition phase of Quicksort. One of the simplest, attributed to Nico Lomuto, operates as follows.

1. Let the variable **boundary** hold the position that separates the values that are smaller than the pivot from those that are not. Originally, **boundary** is set to the first position in the array where the pivot element resides.

2. Look at each remaining item in the array. If this element is smaller than the pivot value, move it toward the beginning by switching it with the first element after the current **boundary** and then moving **boundary** one position to the right.

3. Switch the first element (that is, the pivot) with the value at position **boundary**. Return this position as the value of the pivot index (denoted by **p** in the preceding diagram).

Using the algorithmic description above, write a Java implementation of Quicksort. For further explanation of the procedure, you can consult Jon Bentley's "Programming Pearls" section of the April 1984 issue of *Communications of the ACM*.

Recursive Backtracking

A mighty maze! but not without a plan.
—Alexander Pope, *An Essay on Man,* 1733

Of those areas that make up computer science, the one that tends to capture the most popular attention is artificial intelligence. The idea that a machine could be endowed with the capacity for thought is enticing to some and profoundly disturbing to others. Prior to the advent of modern computers, the debate over artificial intelligence and its potential was primarily philosophical. With the development of extremely fast machines, computers can now perform complex tasks that seem to require intelligence.

Systems that seek to simulate intelligent behavior often make extensive use of recursion, which provides a powerful framework for searching through a set of possibilities for an optimal choice. The general strategy is called **recursive backtracking.** It consists of having the computer make tentative choices in a way that allows it to backtrack to previous decision points so that it can explore other possible options. This chapter presents two applications of recursive backtracking: (1) finding a path through a maze, and (2) choosing a move in a strategy game.

8.1 Backtracking through a Maze

As at most conferences, the participants at the 1979 National Computer Conference in New York City spent much of their time attending technical sessions and surveying the new tools of the trade. That year, however, a special event made the conference much more exciting—the first "Amazing Micro-Mouse Maze Contest," sponsored by IEEE/Spectrum. The engineering teams that entered the contest had built mechanical "mice" whose mission was to perform the classic demonstration of rodent intelligence—running a maze.

Although the idea of building a mechanical mouse brings up a wide range of interesting engineering problems (such as how it should move or sense its environment), the maze-solving aspect of the problem is interesting in its own right. Suppose, for example, that you want to write a Java program to solve mazes like the one in the following diagram:

Such a maze consists of a rectangular array of smaller squares, which can be either empty (representing a corridor section) or filled in (representing a wall). In addition, two of the squares are labeled with the letters '**S**' and '**F**', representing the start and finish squares, respectively.

Let's imagine that you are a programmer in the original Micro-Mouse contest. From an algorithmic perspective, the central problem is to find a way to generate a solution path. More specifically, your mission is to construct a program that, given a representation of this maze as input, will generate a diagram in which one of the possible solution paths is marked.

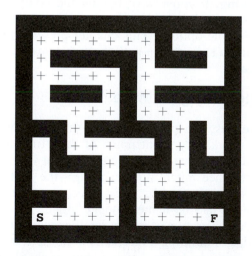

To develop an algorithm for solving a maze, you will need to adopt a systematic approach that explores every possible path until it finds a solution. Since some of the paths lead to dead ends, the process of exploring those paths will necessarily require "backing up" when no further progress is possible. For example, if you begin by going two squares forward from the starting position, you reach a point where you must choose between two possible paths. Such a square will be called a **choice point** in the subsequent discussion.

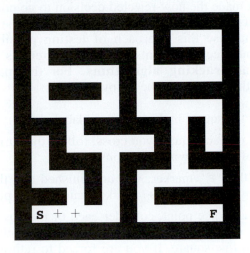

At this point in the maze, you must choose one of the two possible paths for an initial exploration, and, if that route proves unsuccessful, return to this choice point to try the other. Looking down on the maze from above, it is clear that you should continue east and not north, since the latter direction quickly takes you to a dead end. Any program that you write to solve this problem, however, will be forced to explore this path until it actually reaches the dead end.

If your program is unlucky enough to choose the north path first, it will explore ahead until it reaches the following position and notes that it can no longer proceed:

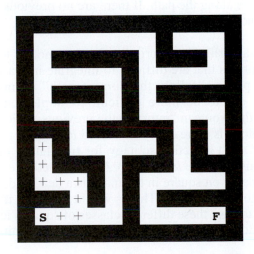

When this situation occurs, your program must enter a backtracking phase, during which it moves backward along its original path until it reaches an earlier choice point. Here, for example, the program must back up to the junction at which it made the now-rejected decision to go north. At that choice point, it must now try the east path and proceed toward an eventual solution.

Algorithms that use this approach of testing possible solutions and returning to previous decision points when such attempts fail are generally referred to as **backtracking algorithms.** For the maze problem, the backtracking algorithm consists of the following steps:

1. Start initially at the square in the maze grid labeled `'s'`.

2. Drawing a `'+'` on each square you cross, follow the current path until you encounter one of the following situations:

    (a) If you hit the `'F'` marker, you are finished and the correct path is indicated by the chain of `'+'` markers currently in place.

    (b) If you hit a choice point, consider each of the possible directions in some fixed order. Repeat this process along that path until you are told to return to this square. If you are forced to return, choose the next possible direction. If you end up attempting all the possible directions without finding a solution, the entire set of passages beyond this point represents a dead end, and you should proceed as in step (d).

    (c) If you hit a square that has already been marked, then the maze contains a loop. To avoid going around that loop forever, it is essential to consider this situation a dead end, and follow the instructions for case (d).

    (d) If you hit a dead end, return to the previous choice point and try the next possible direction. As you backtrack to the choice point, erase the `'+'` markers along the path. If there are no previous choice points, the maze has no solution.

Although this algorithmic description is easy enough to understand, it is based on several notions that are difficult to integrate into a working program. For example, the phrase "follow the current path" seems straightforward enough, but turns out to be more difficult to implement than it sounds. Similarly, the idea that you can "return to the previous choice point and try the next possible direction" is more easily expressed in English than in Java.

Ironically, the most effective strategy for translating this algorithm into Java involves making it a little *less* clever. As presented, the algorithm must be able to tell whether a given square in the maze is a dead end, a choice point, or a corridor square along some path. Things would be easier if you could design the algorithm so as to treat these different classes of squares identically. And, in fact, you can. To do so, the first simplification is to eliminate the notion of dead-end squares by letting the program "bump into" the walls. If your program takes a step forward and finds that the current position is now on a wall square, then the program can conclude that motion is impossible in that direction. You can reduce the complexity further by considering *every* open square in the maze to be a choice point with exactly four possible paths. Some of these paths, of course, run directly into walls, but it is far easier to treat each of these cases in the same way.

It helps to consider these design choices in the context of a very simple maze. Except for its size, the following maze is similar to the earlier example. The only structural difference is that the start position has been replaced by a small diamond that indicates the position of the "current square."

As suggested by the earlier discussion, every square in this maze is a choice point with exit paths leading north, east, south, and west. If you try these directions in that order, the next position to consider is the one you reach by moving northward one square. Taking that step to the north leaves you in the following state:

From this new square, the algorithm must once again try each of the four directions, starting with north. In this case, however, the northward path is less successful since it leads to the following configuration:

In this figure, the fact that the diamond indicating the current square is now sitting on top of a wall means that the algorithm cannot proceed in this direction and must retreat to the preceding position, which looks like this:

Now that moving north has proven to be unproductive, it is time to explore the next possible direction and try moving east. Unfortunately, this option is no better, and it is necessary to retreat once more and try south. In this case, the algorithm encounters a square that is already marked, indicating that the route has doubled back onto a previous path. Given that there is no point in reexploring old territory (particularly since the program is likely to get stuck in a loop this way), the algorithm rejects this direction as well and tries the remaining one. Only when moving west proves to be equally unsuccessful can the algorithm conclude that it has exhausted all options along this route. Failure to find a solution along the path forces the algorithm to back up one more square, bringing things back to the initial configuration:

   The difference between this situation and the original position is that the algorithm has now explored and rejected the northward path. Having done so, it is time to try the next direction by moving east. On the whole, this choice proves more profitable, and, after banging into several more walls, the algorithm reaches the final configuration

   The interesting part of the process of implementing this algorithm in Java lies in finding a straightforward way to manage the backtracking involved in the solution strategy. Somehow, the program must keep track, not only of the current position, but also what directions have been tried at each choice point. This is where recursion comes in handy.

   For recursion to be useful in solving this problem, there must be some way to express the problem of solving a maze in terms of solutions to simpler mazes. To see how this idea might apply, it is again helpful to consider a specific maze, as follows:

If your goal is to think about this problem recursively, you can't look ahead all the way to the solution. What you have to do instead is find a way to redefine the problem so that it is at least slightly simpler. But what does simpler mean in the context of solving a maze? From a human perspective, the difficulty of a particular maze is at least somewhat subjective, but subjective assessments of difficulty are not appropriate for an algorithmic solution. In order to find a recursive decomposition, you need to find some property of the maze that becomes smaller at each stage of the recursive decomposition. Such a property is often called a **metric,** since it serves as a quantitative measure of difficulty.

In the case of a maze, a useful candidate for such a metric is the number of open corridor spaces in the maze. If the number of open spaces gets smaller and smaller, you must eventually either find a solution or eliminate the open space altogether. The key insight that supports the recursive decomposition is that the maze

has a solution if and only if at least one of the following mazes can be solved:

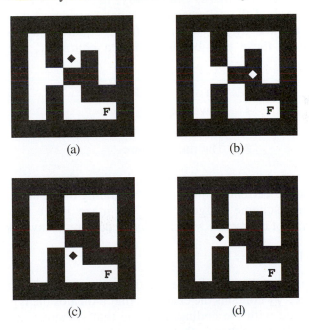

(a)   (b)

(c)   (d)

The four mazes shown in this diagram are simply the original maze, with the starting square replaced by a wall and the new starting position shifted in each of the four compass directions. Each one of these mazes has one less open square than the original and is therefore "simpler" according to that metric. Since three of the four resulting mazes are now unsolvable, it is clear that the mazes are simpler only in the context of this metric and not in the sense of being closer to the exit of the underlying maze.

Actually, it is not necessary to construct a full-fledged wall in the original position. If you instead simply mark the space with a `'+'` as in the earlier diagrams, that marker will suffice as long as you treat the square as identical to a wall as you proceed through the recursion. Moreover, if you mark each square with a `'+'` and unmark it only after you have tried all four directions from that square, then the `'+'` signs in the final maze will indicate the solution path.

For the recursive decomposition to be effective, the process must eventually result in simple cases that allow the recursion to terminate. For the most part, the simple cases are the same as those given in the following informal algorithmic description:

(a)   If the current square is marked with an `'F'`, then a solution has been found.

(b)   If the current square is a wall square or is already marked with a `'+'`, then no path exists in this direction.

Before you try to code this algorithm in Java, you need to choose a data structure to represent the maze. Graphically, the maze is a two-dimensional array in which each of the cells can be an open corridor, a wall, a previously visited square marked by a `'+'`, or the finish square. You can more easily represent each of these possibilities using a character, according to the following code:

> `' '`   An open corridor square
> `'#'`   A wall square
> `'+'`   A previously marked square
> `'F'`   The finish square

The start square need not be represented explicitly in the matrix, since it is used only to establish the current position at the beginning of the algorithm.

This coding scheme suggests that the maze itself is simply a two-dimensional array of characters, which you can declare in Java like this:

```
char[][] maze;
```

If **x** and **y** represent the coordinates of the current position, then the array element **maze[x, y]** contains the character that indicates the type of square.

To get started with the coding, imagine that someone has supplied you with a method called **readMaze** that reads in the data structures for the maze, storing the results in the two-dimensional array **maze** and the integer variables **x0** and **y0**, which specify the starting position. Your mission is to write a method **solveMaze** that searches the data structure for a solution path. The **solveMaze** method takes the coordinates of the current position within the maze and returns a **boolean** value that indicates whether or not the maze is solvable from that position. Thus, the main program that used **solveMaze** might include the following code:

```
if (solveMaze(x0, y0)) {
   printMaze();
} else {
   println("The maze has no solution");
}
```

The code for **solveMaze** is surprisingly easy to write, given the general outline of a solution strategy presented earlier in this chapter. A psuedocode implementation of **solveMaze** looks like this:

```
boolean solveMaze(int x, int y) {
      if (the current square is the finish square)  {
         return true;
      } else if (the current square is a wall or already marked)  {
         return false;
      } else {
         Mark the current square with a plus sign.
         Recursively try each of the four directions; if any succeed, return true.
         Unmark the current square.
         return false;
      }
}
```

None of the italicized English portions of the pseudocode turns out to be at all difficult to code, which makes it easy to produce the complete implementation:

```
boolean solveMaze(int x, int y) {
    if (maze[x][y] == 'F') {
       return true;
    } else if (maze[x][y] == '#' || maze[x][y] == '+') {
       return false;
    } else {
       maze[x][y] = '+';
       if (solveMaze(x, y + 1)) return true;
       if (solveMaze(x + 1, y)) return true;
       if (solveMaze(x, y - 1)) return true;
       if (solveMaze(x - 1, y)) return true;
       maze[x][y] = ' ';
       return false;
    }
}
```

8.2 Strategic Games

In 1769, the Hungarian inventor Wolfgang von Kempelen developed a machine that, from all outward appearances, represented a remarkable advance in engineering. Christened "The Turk," the machine consisted of a life-sized figure (complete with turban and Turkish attire) seated behind a chessboard. Accompanied by the requisite grinding of gears and sliding of rods, The Turk would play exhibition matches during which it displayed great proficiency at the game. Brought to the United States in 1826 by Johann Maelzel (more widely known for his invention of the metronome), The Turk was given to the Chinese Museum in Philadelphia, where it was eventually destroyed by a fire that devastated much of the museum's collection.

On closer examination, The Turk's success as a chess player was revealed to be somewhat less remarkable, since it depended on the human chess player hidden inside. One of the most detailed accounts of this hoax was provided in 1836 by Edgar Allen Poe, who wrote an essay entitled "Maelzel's Chess Player" outlining his suspicions about its operation:

> There is a man, Schlumberger [who is] about the medium
> size, and has a remarkable stoop in the shoulders. Whether
> he professes to play chess or not, we are not informed. It is
> quite certain, however, that he is never to be seen during the
> exhibition of the Chess-Player, although frequently visible
> just before and after the exhibition.

Since that time, of course, technology has proceeded apace. With modern computers, the idea of a chess-playing machine is no longer outlandish, particularly since 1997, when IBM's Deep Blue program beat Gary Kasparov, the reigning human chess champion, in a six-game match. The basic strategy used in Deep Blue, as in all commercially available chess programs, is to look ahead as many moves as possible (given constraints of time) to see which moves in the current position lead to the best positions down the road. Such an approach is called a **lookahead strategy** and is applicable to a wide variety of games.

In many respects, playing a strategy game is similar to solving a maze. Each move constitutes a choice point that leads to a different game path. Some of those paths lead to victory, others to defeat. A program that attempts to play such games intelligently must explore each path to discover which options offer the best chances for victory.

Although games like chess and checkers are probably more exciting, it is easier to illustrate the general structure of game-playing programs in the context of a simpler game. For this purpose, one of the best examples is the game of Nim, which is elementary enough to analyze in detail.

The name Nim, derived from the Middle English verb *nimen* (meaning "to take" or "to steal"), applies to a variety of "take-away" games. One of the most widely known versions is 3-4-5 Nim, which is played with twelve pennies arranged to form three horizontal rows, as shown:

Playing alternately, each of two players then takes away any number of pennies from any one of the horizontal rows. The object of the game is to take the last coin.

For example, the first player (Player A) might take away all five pennies from the last row, leaving the position

Player B must then remove pennies from one of the first two rows. Thus, Player B might take two coins from the first row, leaving the position

Looking at this arrangement, it is not difficult to see that the best move for Player A is to take three of the coins from the second row. This results in the situation

Row 1:

Row 2:

Row 3:

Player B must now take one of the two remaining coins, and Player A wins by taking the other.

Even though Player A eventually discovered a winning move in the position 1-4-0 (that is, the position with three pennies in the first row, one in the second, and none in the third), each player had already thrown away a winning opportunity. Starting with the 3-4-5 arrangement, the first player can always win by making the right sequence of moves. After Player A took all five coins from the last row, however, Player B had an opportunity to win the game by making the correct response. Before reading further, try to see if you can determine the mistake that each player made and devise a winning strategy.

After playing a few games, it becomes clear that some positions are much more promising than others. Using examples from the earlier game, the position 1-1-0 is fatal if the next move happens to be yours. You must take one of the two coins, leaving your opponent free to take the other. On the other hand, the configuration 1-4-0 is an advantageous position from which to move, because taking three coins from the second row leaves your *opponent* in the 1-1-0 position. Since this position will guarantee a loss for your opponent, it must be good for you.

The discovery that Nim has "good" and "bad" positions makes it possible to derive an algorithmic strategy for Nim, since it allows us to differentiate between "good" and "bad" moves. Intuitively, a move is "good" if it leaves your opponent with a "bad" position. Similarly, a position is "bad" if it offers no "good" moves.

Although it may seem surprising at first, these definitions provide pretty much everything you need to write a program to play a winning game of Nim. The key is to take the informal definitions of "good move" and "bad position" and turn them into recursive routines. Just as these concepts are defined in terms of the other, each of the two routines will call the other in order to complete its operation.

Before turning to the details of the implementation, it is useful to define the data structures involved. First of all, there must be some data structure that represents the current state of the game. A position in Nim is completely defined by the number of pennies in each row, which means that an array of integers can be used to represent any position. The other data structure you need is one that represents a move. In Nim, a move is defined by two values:

the number of coins taken and the row number from which they come. Thus, two integers—the number of coins and a row number—are sufficient to represent a move.

Although it would certainly be possible to use these basic structures to represent the state of a Nim game and a move in the game, doing so does not take optimal advantage of the object-oriented capabilities of Java. These two structures—the state of the game and a move—have conceptual integrity that suggests encapsulating each as an object. The easier of the two structures to define is a move, which can be represented in Java using the **NimMove** class shown in Figure 8-1. The class definition allows clients to construct a new move from its components, to obtain the number of coins and row number using the methods **getNCoins** and **getRow**, and to display the move in a human-readable form by redefining its **toString** method.

The class to represent the game state, which appears in Figure 8-2, is somewhat more interesting. The constructor for the **NimState** does not restrict the game to the 3-4-5 variety but allows any number of rows, with any number of coins in each row. The argument to the constructor is an integer array containing the initial number of coins in each row, so the standard game could be constructed as follows:

```
int[] standardNim = { 3, 4, 5 };
NimState state = new NimState(standardNim);
```

The **NimState** class includes several simple methods that support the operations required to implement the game. It includes, for example, a method **isGameOver** that tests whether the last coin has been taken. It also includes the method

```
public void makeMove(NimMove move) {
    rows[move.getRow()] -= move.getNCoins();
}
```

which implements the operation of making a move, which consists of subtracting the specified number of coins from the appropriate row. To support the backtracking necessary for a recursive solution, the **NimState** class also includes the symmetric method

```
public void retractMove(NimMove move) {
    rows[move.getRow()] += move.getNCoins();
}
```

that undoes the **makeMove** operation.

Figure 8-1. The NimMove class

```
/* Class: NimMove */
/**
 * This class encapsulates the data necessary to represent
 * a single move in the game, which for Nim is the number
 * of coins and the row from which they come.
 */
class NimMove {

/* Constructor: NimMove(nCoins, row) */
/**
 * Creates a new NimMove object.
 */
   public NimMove(int nCoins, int row) {
      this.nCoins = nCoins;
      this.row = row;
   }

/* Method: getNCoins() */
/**
 * Returns the number of coins associated with a Nim move.
 */
   public int getNCoins() {
      return nCoins;
   }

/* Method: getRow() */
/**
 * Returns the row number from which the coins are taken.
 */
   public int getRow() {
      return row;
   }

/* Method: toString() */
/**
 * Returns a string representation of a move.
 */
   public String toString() {
      return nCoins + " from row " + row;
   }

/* Private state */
   private int row;
   private int nCoins;

}
```

Figure 8-2. The NimState class

```
/* Class: NimState */
/**
 * This class encapsulates the data necessary to represent
 * the state of the game.  For Nim, the state is simply
 * the number of coins in each row.
 */
class NimState {

/* Constructor: NimState(initialState) */
/**
 * Creates a new NimState object initialized to the values
 * given in the array initialState.
 */
   public NimState(int[] initialState) {
      rows = new int[initialState.length + 1];
      for (int i = 0; i < initialState.length; i++) {
         rows[i + 1] = initialState[i];
      }
   }

/* Method: isGameOver() */
/**
 * Returns true if the game has reached its final state,
 * which for Nim occurs when all the coins are taken.
 */
   public boolean isGameOver() {
      for (int i = 1; i < rows.length; i++) {
         if (rows[i] > 0) return false;
      }
      return true;
   }

/* Method: getMoves() */
/**
 * Returns an Iterator that sequences through the legal
 * moves in this position.
 */
   public Iterator getMoves() {
      ArrayList list = new ArrayList();
      for (int row = 1; row < rows.length; row++) {
         for (int nc = 1; nc <= rows[row]; nc++) {
            list.add(new NimMove(nc, row));
         }
      }
      return list.iterator();
   }
```

continued ☞

Figure 8-2. The NimState class (continued)

```
/* Method: makeMove(move) */
/**
 * Changes the state by making the specified move.
 */
   public void makeMove(NimMove move) {
      rows[move.getRow()] -= move.getNCoins();
   }

/* Method: retractMove(move) */
/**
 * Changes the state to reverse the effect of the move.
 */
   public void retractMove(NimMove move) {
      rows[move.getRow()] += move.getNCoins();
   }

/* Method: isMoveLegal(move) */
/**
 * Returns true if the specified move is legal.
 */
   public boolean isMoveLegal(NimMove move) {
      int row = move.getRow();
      int nCoins = move.getNCoins();
      if (row < 1 || row >= rows.length) return false;
      if (nCoins < 1 || nCoins > rows[row]) return false;
      return true;
   }

/* Method: toString() */
/**
 * Returns a string representation of the state.
 */
   public String toString() {
      String str = "";
      for (int row = 1; row < rows.length; row++) {
         str += "Row " + row + ":";
         for (int i = 0; i < rows[row]; i++) {
            str += " X";
         }
         str += "\n";
      }
      return str;
   }

/* Private data */
   private int[] rows;

}
```

The most interesting method in the **NimState** class is **getMoves**, which creates a list of the available moves and returns an **Iterator** that sequences through the available possibilities. Thus, to try all the moves in a particular state, you could use a **for** loop that looks like this:

```
for (Iterator i = state.getMoves(); i.hasNext(); ) {
    NimMove move = (NimMove) i.next();
    . . . code to process the move . . .
}
```

Given these definitions for **NimState** and **NimMove**, it is now possible to go back and think about how to design an algorithm to find the best move in a particular situation. To implement the proposed the recursive solution, what you need is two methods that capture the ideas of a "bad" position and a "good" move. In Java, these methods might be

1. A boolean function **isBadPosition(state)** that looks at the position represented by **state** and returns **true** if that position is a losing one, such as 1-1-0.

2. A function **findGoodMove(state)** that returns the best move in a given situation. In some cases, however, there may be no good moves, in which case **findGoodMove** returns **null** to indicate that fact.

Each of these methods operates by calling the other. Since a bad position is one in which there are no good moves, the function **isBadPosition** can simply call **findGoodMove** and test to see whether it returns **null**. Similarly, **findGoodMove** operates by making every possible move until it finds one that leaves the opponent in a position that **isBadPosition** indicates is a losing one.

The one piece of the puzzle that still needs to be specified is the simple case. At some point, **isBadPosition** cannot call **findGoodMove** but must instead decide that a position is bad on its own account. At first glance, it seems that the position 1-1-0 (along with the symmetric positions 1-0-1 and 0-1-1) are the simplest bad positions, but such a choice fails to take account of an even less advantageous situation. Although it is certainly true that these positions are bad for the player to move, but things could be worse—that player could have already lost. If a player is faced with the position 0-0-0, things have already gone badly, because the opponent must have taken the last penny.

Using the case in which the game is already over as the ultimate bad position leads to the following code for **isBadPosition**:

```
private boolean isBadPosition(NimState state) {
    if (state.isGameOver()) return true;
    return findGoodMove(state) == null;
}
```

The code for **findGoodMove** is a little longer, but not any more difficult conceptually.

```
private NimMove findGoodMove(NimState state) {
   for (Iterator i = state.getMoves(); i.hasNext(); ) {
      NimMove move = (NimMove) i.next();
      state.makeMove(move);
      boolean isBadForOpponent = isBadPosition(state);
      state.retractMove(move);
      if (isBadForOpponent) return move;
   }
   return null;
}
```

The idea here is that the **for** loop makes every possible move in order and then evaluates the resulting situation. If **isBadPosition** indicates that this new position would result in a loss for the opponent, the move must have been a good one. In that case, the code takes back the move to restore the original state and then returns the successful move as the value of the method. If not, it takes the move back and moves on to try the next. If the program get all the way to the end of the **for** loop without discovering a good move, **findGoodMove** returns **null** to indicate its failure to find a winning move.

The technique used to solve the Nim game is applicable to most two-handed strategy games, at least in theory. The difficulty with this approach is that most games are so complex that it takes far too long to carry through with this analysis to any significant depth. For any game of reasonable complexity, a program is forced to limit the number of positions that it analyzes before making its turn.

In chess, for example, a player ordinarily has approximately 32 options at each turn. In response to each of these moves, the opponent has 32 possible replies, which amounts to roughly 1000 positions after a single pair of moves. Since the average chess game involves about 40 moves for each player, the total number of different lines of play is therefore

$$1000^{40} = 10^{120}$$

This number is so preposterously large that, if a trillion computers on each of a trillion different planets were each able to analyze a trillion positions every second, it would still take more than

$$10^{75} \text{ years}$$

just to determine the best opening move!

In light of the enormous number of possibilities in a complete game, it is usually necessary to reduce this complexity by limiting the number of moves the program looks ahead and by eliminating unattractive variations relatively early.

Exercises

8-1. In the maze-solving program presented in this chapter, the program unmarks each square as it retreats while backtracking. Removing the marks from the blind alleys that the program tries along the way ensures that the final path will be displayed correctly. However, if the goal is to find the finish square in the shortest possible time, it is more efficient to leave these markers in place. Discuss how this change affects the efficiency of the algorithm. In what situations would this new approach improve the program's performance?

8-2. Instead of awarding the game to the player who takes the last coin, Nim can also be played "in reverse" so that the player who takes the last coin *loses*. Redesign the strategy routines so that they give the correct moves for this "Reverse Nim" game, making as few changes to the existing code as you can.

8-3. In the implementation of Nim used in the text, the simple case test included in **isBadPosition** is not strictly necessary, and the method could have been written more simply as

```
private boolean isBadPosition(NimState state) {
    return findGoodMove(state) == null;
}
```

Why does this simplication work in this case?

8-4. The algorithm presented in this chapter to solve the Nim game is quite inefficient because it must analyze the same position many different times. For example, if the computer plays first from the 3-4-5 position, making the first move requires 25,771 calls to **isBadPosition**. Since the total number of possible positions is only 120, this number of calls seems excessive. You can improve the efficiency of the solution dramatically by having the program keep track of the result each time it analyzes a position. In the Nim game, for example, you can construct a table with one entry for each of the possible positions so that each entry indicates whether that position is "good," "bad," or "undetermined." Whenever you analyze a particular position in the course of the game, you can simply store the result in the table. The next time the program calls **isBadPosition**, it can simply return the information stored in the table. Write a complete program for the Nim game, using this extension. Try your program with longer initial rows. How quickly does it seem to operate?

8-5.   As presented, the recursive strategy discussed in the text is not directly applicable to games in which draws are possible, since one can no longer classify all positions as good or bad. On the other hand, it is reasonably simple to adapt the strategy to handle draws by replacing **isBadPosition** with a **ratePosition** method that examines a position and assigns it a numerical score. For example, a simple assignment would be to use -1 to represent a losing position, +1 to represent a winning position, and 0 to represent one that leads to a draw. As before, the recursive insight is that the best move is the one that leaves the opponent in the worst position. Furthermore, the worst position is the one that offers the least promising best move. Since the goal is to select a move that minimizes the opponent's best opportunity, this strategy is called the **minimax algorithm.** Using this expanded strategy, write a program that plays a perfect game of Tic-Tac-Toe. In your implementation, the human player should make the first move, and the program should make the optimum reply.

8-6.   Before Rubik made all other cube-based puzzles seem pointless by comparison, many toy departments carried a puzzle with four painted cubes, marketed under the name of "Instant Insanity." The cube faces were painted with the colors green, white, blue, and red (symbolized as **G**, **W**, **B**, and **R** in the diagrams), and each of the four cubes was composed of a distinct arrangement of colors. "Unfolding" the cubes makes it possible to show the color patterns.

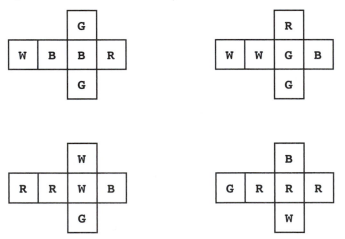

The object of the puzzle was to arrange these cubes into a line so that each line of four faces contained one face of each color. Write a program to solve "Instant Insanity" by backtracking.

8-7.   In the game of chess, most of the pieces move in relatively conventional patterns along horizontal, vertical, or diagonal lines. The knight is an exception to this otherwise orderly pattern and moves in a rather unusual way. From its starting point, the knight moves two squares in any direction, horizontally or vertically, and then moves one square at a right angle to the original direction of motion. Thus, the knight shown below can move to any of the eight black squares indicated by a diamond:

Even though its motion seems rather limited, the knight certainly gets around and can reach all sixty-four squares on the chessboard in as many moves. A series of knight's moves that traverses an entire chessboard without ever landing on the same square twice is known as a **knight's tour.** For example, the following diagram shows a knight's tour that returns to its initial square on the sixty-fourth move:

24	27	10	5	12	31	16	7
21	4	23	26	9	6	13	32
28	25	20	11	30	15	8	17
3	22	29	36	19	56	33	14
42	63	38	55	48	35	18	57
39	2	41	60	37	52	47	34
62	43	64	49	54	45	58	51
1	40	61	44	59	50	53	46

Write a Java program to find a knight's tour on an 8×8 chessboard, using a backtracking algorithm similar to the one used in **solveMaze**. Although the simple backtracking algorithm used to solve the maze in this chapter is sufficient to solve the knight's tour problem in theory, it consumes far too much computation time to be practicable. Therefore, if you intend to test this program, you must improve its algorithmic performance. One approach is to use a separate matrix to keep track of the number of squares from which any particular square can be reached. If making any move results in isolating some other square, then no solution is possible, and the program can immediately reject this possibility.

Graphical Applications

Dost thou love pictures?
—William Shakespeare, *The Taming of the Shrew*, 1594

In teaching almost any discipline, one quickly comes to appreciate the truth of the old saying that "a picture is worth a thousand words." As a means of expressing a general concept, a simple diagram often conveys far more than many pages of descriptive text. In computer science, however, this adage has another interpretation—a program that generates a picture is often a thousand times more captivating and exciting than one whose output is limited to words or numbers.

There are many applications in computer graphics in which recursion plays an important role. In Chapter 1, one of the first examples used to illustrate the idea of recursion was the problem of generating "computer art" reminiscent of Mondrian's style:

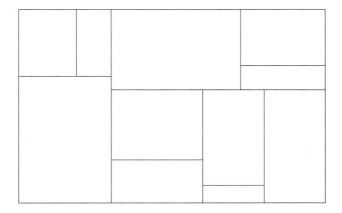

In this example, the complete picture is produced by dividing the original rectangle into parts which are, in turn, recursively subdivided until the program determines that the units are small enough to remain undivided.

9.1 Computer Graphics in Java

Writing a program to generate designs of this sort requires more than an understanding of its recursive structure. To see these programs work and thereby experience some of the excitement of computer graphics, you need to learn how to display graphical patterns on your computer. Java's libraries offer extensive graphical capabilities through its standard application programmer interfaces (APIs), but these facilities are often difficult for novices to use and are not well suited for drawing recursive patterns. To get around these problems, the programs in this chapter make use of the **GPen** class, which is defined in the **acm.graphics** package developed by the Association for Computing Machinery (ACM) for pedagogical use. The methods in the **GPen** class that you need to know are

- **setLocation(x, y)**, which moves the pen to the specified location without drawing a line
- **drawLine(dx, dy)**, which draws a line starting at the current pen position and extending **dx** units horizontally and **dy** units vertically
- **drawPolarLine(r, theta)**, which draws a line from the current pen position whose length is **r** units and which moves in the direction **theta**, measured in degrees counterclockwise from the $+x$ axis.

As in the traditional Java libraries, the coordinate system is measured in pixels, with x values increasing to the right and y values increasing downward.

To get a better sense of the operation of these methods, imagine that you are using a pen on a large piece of graph paper marked off in pixels, with position $(0, 0)$ in the upper left-hand corner. Invoking the method

```
pen.setLocation(x, y)
```

corresponds to picking up the pen and moving it to a new position, indicated by the **x** and **y** parameters. A call to

```
pen.drawLine(dx, dy)
```

corresponds to drawing a line with the pen whose vector displacements are given by **dx** and **dy**. Thus, a call to

```
pen.drawLine(100, -50)
```

draws a line segment by moving the pen 100 pixels right and 50 pixels up from its previous location.

Subsequent calls to **drawLine** begin where the last line left off, which makes it easy to generate shapes composed of connected line segments. As an example, the rectangular box

can be drawn using the following sequence of method calls:

```
pen.setLocation(50, 50);
pen.drawLine(100, 0);
pen.drawLine(0, 50);
pen.drawLine(-100, 0);
pen.drawLine(0, -50);
```

9.2 Fractal Geometry

In his essay "On Poetry—A Rhapsody" written in 1735, Jonathan Swift offers the following observation on the continuity of natural processes:

> So, naturalists observe, a flea
> Hath smaller fleas that on him prey;
> And these have smaller still to bite 'em
> And so proceed, *ad infinitum*.

Taking a large amount of anatomical license, one can illustrate this process by representing an idealized flea as an equilateral triangle, shown here under considerable magnification:

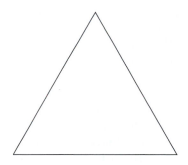

Putting a smaller flea on each of the two segments that form the back of the large flea illustrates the next stage in Swift's progression:

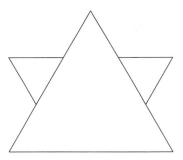

Each of these two new fleas can then play host to two smaller fleas, which leads to the following menagerie:

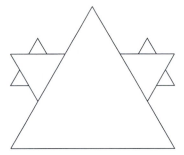

Clearly, this process can be repeated (as Swift suggests) *ad infinitum* with progressively tinier fleas.

Patterns such as this one have considerable mathematical significance and are known collectively as **fractals.** The term *fractal* was coined in 1975 by Benoit Mandelbrot, who synthesized several earlier mathematical discoveries to create a new geometry of fractal patterns. The principal defining characteristic of a fractal is that the components of a figure retain the same shape regardless of their size. In the case of the flea diagram, for example, each flea has exactly the same shape as the larger flea on which it sits. As it turns out, this repetition of similar structures at varying scales and the characteristic roughness of shape make fractals an excellent model for many of nature's irregularities.

The classic example used to illustrate how fractal geometry applies to nature is the problem of determining the length of a coastline. The answer to this question depends on how closely you look. Conventional satellite photography reveals comparatively little detail, and any measurement based on such photographs will fail to account for peninsulas and inlets that are too small to be seen at that scale. With higher resolution, certain features may become visible, but there will always be still smaller aberrations in the coastline (peninsulas on peninsulas in much the same manner as Swift's fleas) that escape notice.

Before turning to the how fractals relate to recursive programming, it helps to modify the "nested fleas" example to produce a figure that is somewhat more uniform in its structure. Once again, the figure begins with an equilateral triangle:

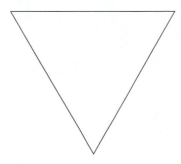

This figure represents the initial stage in the construction of a pattern called the Koch fractal, after the mathematician Helge von Koch. The next step in the construction consists of replacing each of the line segments in the figure with one that includes a triangular wedge in its center, like this:

The first phase of this construction, therefore, replaces all three edges of the original triangle with this bumpy line to obtain the following figure:

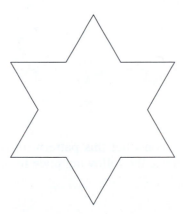

Fractals are categorized according to the number of levels at which such replacement operations are performed, which is called the **order** of the fractal. The original triangle is the Koch fractal of order 0, and the six-pointed star is the Koch fractal of order 1.

The process can be repeated to generate increasingly complex figures. If, for example, you replace the center of *each* line segment in the order 1 fractal with a smaller triangular wedge, you get the Koch fractal of order 2:

Repeating this process one more time produces the "snowflake" curve of order 3:

Writing a program to construct this pattern turns out to be surprisingly simple. As a start, you can use the following code to draw the original order-0 fractal:

```
void drawOrder0Fractal(double len) {
   double cx = getWidth() / 2;
   double cy = getHeight() / 2;
   double x0 = cx - len / 2 * GMath.cosDegrees(60);
   double y0 = cy - len / 2 * GMath.sinDegrees(60);
   pen.setLocation(x0, y0);
   pen.drawPolarLine(len, 0);
   pen.drawPolarLine(len, -120);
   pen.drawPolarLine(len, +120);
}
```

The first two lines in this method set **cx** and **cy** to the coordinates of the center of the window; the next two use trigonometry to compute the coordinates of the starting point for the triangle, which is the leftmost vertex in this example. (The **sinDegrees** and **cosDegrees** methods compute the sine and cosine of an angle measured in degrees and are supplied as part of the **GMath** class in the ACM libraries). From that point, drawing the triangle is easy, particularly since the **GPen** class includes the **drawPolarLine** method. The first line in the triangle extends straight across toward the right, which is the 0-degree direction. The next continues at an angle of 120 degrees clockwise from the first, and the final line extends at an angle of 120 degrees clockwise from the horizontal, thereby closing the triangle.

To reach the next level, you must replace each of these straight lines with a fractal line of the form

To draw this fractal line from the starting point at the left edge, the **GPen** object (1) draws a line in the same direction as the original, but only for one third of its length, (2) turns 60 degrees to the right and draws another line of this same distance, (3) turns 60 degrees in the opposite direction from the original line to draw the other half of the wedge, and (4) completes the figure with a line segment in the original direction. You can therefore implement the entire operation as follows:

```
void drawFractalLine(double len, int theta) {
   pen.drawPolarLine(len / 3, theta);
   pen.drawPolarLine(len / 3, theta + 60);
   pen.drawPolarLine(len / 3, theta - 60);
   pen.drawPolarLine(len / 3, theta);
}
```

This method makes it possible to draw the order-1 fractal by replacing each of the calls to **drawPolarLine** in the **drawOrder0Fractal** method with a call to `drawFractalLine`, as follows:

```
void drawOrder1Fractal(double len) {
   double cx = getWidth() / 2;
   double cy = getHeight() / 2;
   double x0 = cx - len / 2 * GMath.cosDegrees(60);
   double y0 = cy - len / 2 * GMath.sinDegrees(60);
   pen.setLocation(x0, y0);
   pen.drawFractalLine(len, 0);
   pen.drawFractalLine(len, -120);
   pen.drawFractalLine(len, +120);
}
```

At this point, you could go on to create the order-2 and the order-3 fractals by adding additional nested procedures, but this strategy would fail to take advantage of the power of recursion. What you would like instead is to write a single method that allows you to draw fractals of any specified order by defining those fractals in terms of simpler ones.

To make this strategy work, you need to recognize the recursive character of `drawFractalLine`. In the general case, drawing a fractal line of order N is simply a matter of drawing four fractal lines of order $N-1$ in the appropriate directions. Thus, each of the calls to `drawPolarLine` in `drawFractalLine` should be replaced by recursive calls to `drawFractalLine` that draw fractal lines of the next smaller order. The only time you need to call `drawPolarLine` is when your task is to draw an order-0 fractal line, which is simply a straight line. This insight leads immediately to a complete recursive solution.

```
void drawFractal(double len, int order) {
   double cx = getWidth() / 2;
   double cy = getHeight() / 2;
   double x0 = cx - len / 2 * GMath.cosDegrees(60);
   double y0 = cy - len / 2 * GMath.sinDegrees(60);
   pen.setLocation(x0, y0);
   pen.drawFractalLine(len, 0, order);
   pen.drawFractalLine(len, -120, order);
   pen.drawFractalLine(len, +120, order);
}

void drawFractalLine(double len, int theta, int order) {
   if (order == 0) {
      pen.drawPolarLine(len, theta);
   } else {
      pen.drawFractalLine(len / 3, theta, order - 1);
      pen.drawFractalLine(len / 3, theta + 60, order - 1);
      pen.drawFractalLine(len / 3, theta - 60, order - 1);
      pen.drawFractalLine(len / 3, theta, order - 1);
   }
}
```

Exercises

9-1.   Once upon a time, there was a sensible straight line who
was hopelessly in love with a dot.

With these words, we are introduced to the hero of Norton Juster's
delightful story *The Dot and the Line,* who eventually discovers the
versatility of his linear form and lives "if not happily ever after, at least
reasonably so." As a way of demonstrating his newfound talents to the
object of his affection, the Line assumes the following form:

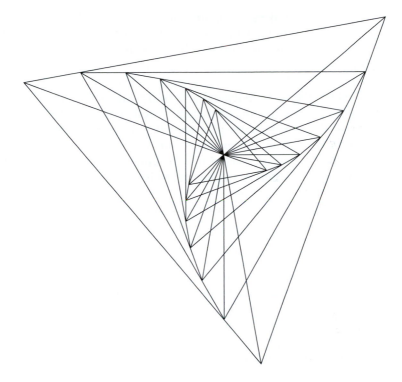

Taking advantage of the fact that this diagram consists of several
repetitions of the figure

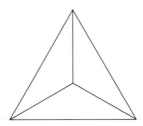

drawn at various sizes and angles, write a Java program to generate the diagram. In this example, although recursion is not strictly necessary, it provides a simple way of generating the repeated figures.

9-2.   Using the definitions of **setLocation** and **drawLine** as given in this chapter, complete the code for the Mondrian-style painting program described in Chapter 1. The difficulty lies in choosing some criterion for terminating the recursion. Ideally, the decision of whether to split a subcanvas should depend on the size of the canvas in some way; larger problems should be subdivided more often than smaller ones.

9-3.   Modify the **drawFractal** program to generate the flea diagrams used in this text. Although the figures are similar in structure to the Koch fractal, the need to retrace interior lines adds some interesting complexity.

9-4.   In the text, the scale-independence of fractals is described in terms of the problem of coastline measurement. Fractals can also be used to generate random coastal patterns in a way that illustrates their application to natural phenomena. For example, suppose that you wanted to generate a random stretch of coastline, linking two points **A** and **B**. The unimaginative solution (using creativity of order 0) is to connect them with a simple straight line.

To give this coastline some semblance of irregularity, you can introduce triangular fractal distortion exactly like that used to generate the snowflake design. The difference is that the choice of direction in which any particular triangle points is random, so that some triangles point up while others point down. Thus, after two levels of fractal decomposition, you might get the line

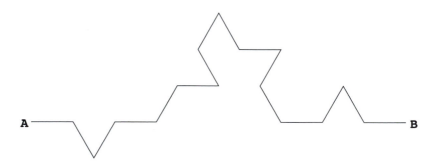

Repeating this process with a fractal of order 5 produces a fairly elaborate coastline that shows almost no trace of the triangular pattern used to generate it:

A 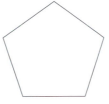 B

Using this general method, write a program that generates a fractal coastline for any given order.

9-5. A visually interesting class of fractals can be constructed as follows. Start with any polygon, such as the pentagon shown below:

At each corner of the figure, draw an identical figure one half the size, outside the original figure, to create the following structure:

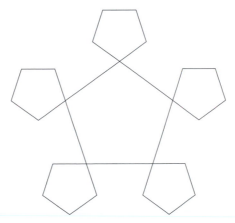

You can use recursion to repeat this process at each of the newly generated corners. Thus the next figure in this process would be

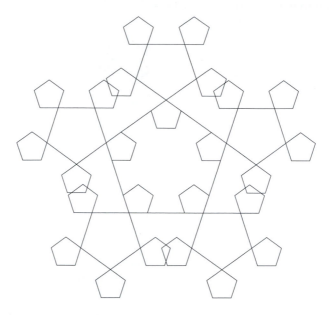

Write a Java program that generates diagrams that follow this rule. In designing your program, you should make it easy to change any of the following:

- The number of sides in the basic figure
- The length of the edge
- The number of recursive levels

Recursive Data

If somebody there chanced to be
Who loved me in a manner true
My heart would point him out to me
And I would point him out to you.
— Gilbert and Sullivan, *Ruddigore,* 1887

One of the important strengths of modern programming languages lies in the flexibility they offer for data representation. Early languages, such as FORTRAN, restricted the user to a small set of primitive data types and arrays. Java programmers have considerably more freedom because the language allows them to define new classes to represent more sophisticated structures. These classes, moreover, can be recursive in that the definition of a class can include references to objects of the same class. Recursive classes of this sort make it possible to apply the power of recursion to data representation in much the same way that recursive methods provide a powerful tool for defining the algorithmic structure of a program.

10.1 Representing Strings as Linked Lists

From your first days as a Java programmer, you have almost certainly had the opportunity to work with the **String** class, which is defined in the **java.lang** package but also supported at the language level through the existence of string constants and the concatenation operator. Java's **String** class is a wonderful tool, primarily because its definition allows you to think about strings as abstract entities without having to be aware of their internal representation. Most other languages, including popular object-oriented languages like C++, force programmers to know much more about the underlying representation of string data, which inevitably makes strings more difficult to use.

As it happens, strings in Java are represented internally as arrays of characters, just as they are in most languages. That design decision, however, was not the only possible choice. Because strings in Java are defined by their abstract behavior and not their representation, the designers of the **java.lang**

133

package could have chosen other representations as long as those representations could provide the same functionality. This section considers the possibility of representing strings as a linked list of characters, not because such a representation makes sense from a pragmatic point of view, but because linked lists provide a simple illustration of a recursive data structure.

A **linked list** is a data structure that represents an ordered list of elements (just as an array does) in which the order of the elements is maintained by an object reference from one element to the one that follows it. The graphical representation of a linked list typically uses arrows to indicate the order of the elements. For example, a linked list consisting of the characters **'A'**, **'B'**, and **'C'** would be drawn like this:

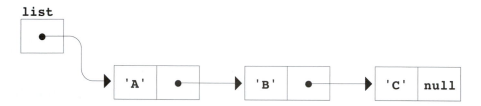

In this diagram, each of the three characters is stored in a data structure that consists of a character and a link to the next such structure in the list. In the context of a linked list, these structures, usually called **cells,** are easily represented in Java using the following class definition:

```
class CharCell {
    char ch;
    CharCell link;
}
```

The definition of **CharCell** is recursive in that one of the components of a **CharCell** object is itself a **CharCell**. At one level, that idea can be confusing. If you think of an object as consisting of its entire collection of parts, it is hard to imagine how one object can contain another object of the same class. For one thing, the outer object would seemingly have to be larger than anything it contains, so there is seemingly a paradox if an object includes something of its own class. For another, the idea that every **CharCell** object contains another **CharCell** seems to suggest nonterminating recursion, given that if that inner **CharCell** contains another **CharCell**, and so on, it is not obvious how such a process can ever stop.

The resolution of this dilemma lies in the fact that objects in Java are represented internally by using the memory address of the object as a **reference.** Relative to objects, which can be of arbitrary size, object references are small, occupying only enough memory space to specify an address. There is no paradox at all in the fact that an object can contain a reference to an object of its own class, since the reference is smaller than the object itself. Similarly, the problem of nontermination goes away because the use of references means that the reference value **null** is available to terminate the recursion. The use of **null** is already suggested by the diagram, where **null** indicates that there are no characters following **'C'** in the list.

Before trying to code operations on character lists, it is important to remember that the original goal of this example was to define a new class that offers the same functionality as the standard **String** class even though it uses a different internal representation. The **CharCell** class itself cannot serve that function; **CharCell** is useful as the internal representation for such a class rather than as the class itself. The string operations themselves must be defined as methods in a new class—called **CLString** in this discussion—that uses **CharCell** to construct its internal representation. The definition for that class will look something like this:

```
public class CLString {

    ... various public methods for the CLString class ...

/* Private state */
    private CharCell list;

}
```

It's important to note that the **CharCell** object used internally to hold the characters in the string is defined to be **private** and therefore inaccessible to clients of the **CLString** class. This protection against having clients look at the internal structure is reinforced by the fact the **CharCell** class itself is not **public** but is instead private to the package that defines it. These design decisions ensure that **CLString** works in the way that the **String** class does, in terms of hiding its internal representation.

If **CLString** is supposed to act as an alternative representation for the built-in **String** class, it must support public methods that match those in the **String** class itself. Defining the full set of methods would defeat the purpose of the example by obscuring the fundamental recursive ideas in a maze of method definitions. To examine how recursive data structures suggest the use of recursive methods to manipulate them, it is sufficient to consider a much smaller set of methods, as follows:

- A constructor **CLString(str)** that creates a **CLString** object from a standard Java string

- An implementation of the **toString()** method that converts a **CLString** back to its traditional Java form

- An implementation of the **length()** method that returns the number of characters in a **CLString**

- An implementation of **concat(s2)**, which concatenates the **CLString s2** onto the end of the **CLString** object on which this method is called

The full implementation of the **CLString** class defines each of these methods as having two parts: a public method that maintains the semantics of the string operation in its traditional form and a private recursive method that actually implements the operation in terms of the underlying data structure. For example, the implementation of the public version of the **length** method is simply

```
public int length() {
   return length(list);
}
```

The body of this method is a call to a private version of the **length** method that takes the instance variable **list** as an argument. That method is in turn defined along the lines suggested by the following pseudocode:

```
private int length(CharCell list) {
   Calculate and return the length of the linked list given by list.
}
```

There are several possible strategies for counting the number of elements in a linked list or for performing the operations required by the other methods. As you will discover in exercise 10-1, you can implement all these operations iteratively in a very straightforward way. The recursive structure of the data, however, suggests an alternative recursive implementation that will reinforce your appreciation for the self-referential aspect of the underlying representation.

Before you consider how you might code the private version of the **length** method, it is useful to begin thinking about strings from a new perspective. You need to dismiss from your mind the notion that a string is an array of characters or even a list of characters represented in some other form. For the moment, imagine that a string is simply one of the two following possibilities:

1. The empty string represented by **null**

2. A character followed by a string

This definition reflects the underlying structure of the **CharCell** class and closely resembles the recursive definition of a noun phrase from Chapter 4.

The advantage of adopting this conceptual definition for a string is that doing so provides an intuitive model for recursive methods that take strings as arguments. The simple case in such routines is always that of the empty string. In the general case, the recursive decomposition consists of dividing a string into its first character and the remainder of the list. This insight, for example, makes it easy to code the private version of the **length** method, which looks like this:

```
private int length(CharCell list) {
    if (list == null) {
        return 0;
    } else {
        return 1 + length(list.link);
    }
}
```

Rendered in English, this implementation operates by noting that (1) the length of the empty string is zero and (2) the length of any other string is one more than the length of that string after taking away its first character.

The private version of **toString** follows much the same form. If the character list is **null**, the corresponding **String** in the traditional Java representation is simply the empty string. For any other string, you can perform the necessary conversion by executing the following informal steps:

1. Divide the character list into its first character and the remainder of the list.

2. Use recursion to convert the remainder of the list to a Java string.

3. Concatenate the first character back onto the front of the result from step 2.

This strategy gives rise to the following implementation of **toString**:

```
public String toString() {
    return toString(list);
}

private String toString(CharCell list) {
    if (list == null) {
        return "";
    } else {
        return list.ch + toString(list.link);
    }
}
```

The **CLString** constructor and the **concat** method require somewhat more effort. The difference between these two methods and simpler methods like **toString** and **length** lies in the fact that both the constructor and the **concat** method must create a new **CLString** object. Despite this added wrinkle, the overall recursive structure is the same.

Consider, for example, the definition of the **concat** method, which concatenates a second **CLString** to the end of the current one. The public version of the method defines the result in terms of a private **concat** method that takes two character lists represented in their internal **CharCell** form:

```
public CLString concat(CLString s2) {
    return new CLString(concat(list, s2.list));
}
```

The private version of **concat** must then take two character lists and return a new character list that contains the characters in the original lists concatenated end to end. For example, if **s1** is the linked list

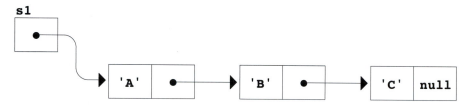

and **s2** is the list

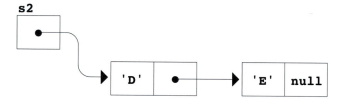

then calling

```
CharCell s3 = concat(s1, s2);
```

should generate a list that looks like this:

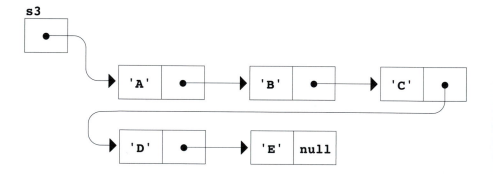

Once again, the recursive nature of the data structure gives rise to a straightforward coding for the **concat** method. Let's consider the two possibilities for the string **s1**. If **s1** is empty, then concatenating **s1** and **s2** leaves only the characters in **s2**. If **s1** is not empty, you can concatenate **s1** and **s2** using the following three-step process, which is almost identical to the strategy used earlier for **toString**.

1. Divide **s1** into its first character and the remainder of the list.
2. Use recursion to concatenate the remainder of **s1** to the front of **s2**.
3. Concatenate the first character back onto the front of the result from step 2.

In this case, the concatenation operation in step 3 consists of creating a new character cell containing the character and the list of the characters that follow it in the combined string. The code for **concat** therefore includes the allocation of a new **CharCell** object and the initialization of its fields, as follows:

```
private CharCell concat(CharCell s1, CharCell s2) {
   if (s1 == null) {
      return s2;
   } else {
      CharCell newCell = new CharCell();
      newCell.ch = s1.ch;
      newCell.link = concat(s1.link, s2);
      return newCell;
   }
}
```

If you think carefully about the operation of **concat**, you will realize that the character cells in the result can be shared with those in other **CLString** objects. In the most recent example, the last two characters in the list labeled **s3** are in fact still part of the internal structure for **s2**. While such sharing of internal structure may initially seem surprising, it turns out to have no effect whatsoever on clients of the **CLString** class. The reason such sharing is permissible grows out of the fact that the Java **String** class—and, symmetrically, the **CLString** simulation of it—are **immutable** types, which means that none of the operations on an object of that class change the underlying representation once the object has been created. If it were possible for clients to change the underlying representation, such sharing would be inappropriate because changes to one structure might result in unexpected changes to other structures that happened to share parts of the internal representation.

The complete code for the **CLString** class appears in Figure 10-1.

Figure 10-1. The CLString class

```
/* Class: CLString */
/**
 * This class provides string operations similar to those
 * in the standard String class, but with a different
 * underlying representation. That representation
 * happens to be a linked list of characters, but
 * clients need not be aware of this fact.
 */

public class CLString {

/* Constructor: CLString(str) */
/**
 * Creates a new CLString from a standard Java string.
 */
   public CLString(String str) {
      list = toCLString(str);
   }

/* Method: toString() */
/**
 * Converts a CLString to a standard Java string.
 */
   public String toString() {
      return toString(list);
   }

/* Method: length() */
/**
 * Returns the number of characters in the CLString.
 */
   public int length() {
      return length(list);
   }

/* Method: concat(s2) */
/**
 * Concatenates a second CLString to the end of this one.
 */
   public CLString concat(CLString s2) {
      return new CLString(concat(list, s2.list));
   }
```

continued ☞

Figure 10-1. The CLString class (continued)

```
/* Private constructor: CLString(list) */
/**
 * Creates a new CLString from a character list.
 */
   private CLString(CharCell list) {
      this.list = list;
   }
/* Private method: toCLString(str) */
/**
 * Creates a character list corresponding to the string.
 */
   private CharCell toCLString(String str) {
      if (str.length() == 0) {
         return null;
      } else {
         CharCell newCell = new CharCell();
         newCell.ch = str.charAt(0);
         newCell.link = toCLString(str.substring(1));
         return newCell;
      }
   }
/* Private method: toString(list) */
/**
 * Converts the character list to a string.
 */
   private String toString(CharCell list) {
      if (list == null) {
         return "";
      } else {
         return list.ch + toString(list.link);
      }
   }
/* Private method: length(list) */
/**
 * Calculates the length of the character list.
 */
   private int length(CharCell list) {
      if (list == null) {
         return 0;
      } else {
         return 1 + length(list.link);
      }
   }
```

continued ☞

Figure 10-1. The CLString class (continued)

```
/* Private method: concat(s1, s2) */
/**
 * Creates a new list by concatenating s1 and s2.
 */
   private CharCell concat(CharCell s1, CharCell s2) {
       if (s1 == null) {
           return s2;
       } else {
           CharCell newCell = new CharCell();
           newCell.ch = s1.ch;
           newCell.link = concat(s1.link, s2);
           return newCell;
       }
   }

/* Private state */

   private CharCell list;

}

/* Private class: CharCell */
/**
 * This class provides the structure definition necessary
 * to store individual cells in a character list.
 */
class CharCell {
   char ch;
   CharCell link;
}
```

10.2 Binary Search Trees

The enormous difference in the performance of the sorting algorithms from Chapter 7 offers a vivid illustration of the importance of algorithmic efficiency. Even with the best algorithms, however, sorting is time-consuming, especially when large amounts of data are involved. In many practical applications, it makes sense to avoid the cost of sorting a large list of items by making sure to insert each item into the correct position at the time you add it to the list. The cost of inserting an item in its proper sequence is larger than, for example, simply adding it to the end, but eliminating the need to sort the list at a later point offers a significant advantage. If nothing else, the cost of keeping the list sorted can be distributed over time, so that the program pays a little of that cost at each insertion rather than paying all at once the cost of sorting the entire list.

Algorithms that distribute time-consuming activities over a series of individual operations are said to **amortize** the cost of those operations.

The task of keeping a list in sorted order as you add new items can be broken down into two distinct operations. The first step is to find the correct position for the new item. This step constitutes the *search* phase of the algorithm. Once you have found the correct position, the next step consists of inserting the new item in that position. This step constitutes the *insert* phase. The efficiency of these two phases turns out to depend dramatically on the data structures used to represent the list. Moreover, a particular data structure may be very efficient for one phase of the operation and yet be highly inefficient for the other.

As an example, think about what happens if you store the items in a sorted array. The array representation makes it easy to implement the search phase efficiently, because the binary search algorithm from Chapter 2 makes it possible to locate the correct position in $O(\log N)$ time. By contrast, the insert phase in an array-based representation is extremely slow. To ensure that the array remains sorted, it is necessary to move the rest of the elements in the entire array one position to the right to make room for the new element. Because this phase of the operation could require moving every element if the new element occurred at the beginning of the array, the worst-case performance for the insert phase is $O(N)$.

If you instead represent the sequence of values using a linked list, the situation is reversed in terms of the computational complexity of its steps. In a linked list, the insert phase of the operation—once you have located the correct position—can be performed in constant time. Unfortunately, the linked list representation makes it impossible to exploit the advantages of binary search, because there is no way to achieve the effect of dividing the list in two.

The computational complexity of the search and insert phases for the array and linked-list representations are summarized in the following table:

	search phase	insert phase	combined search + insert
array	$O(\log N)$	$O(N)$	$O(N)$
linked list	$O(N)$	$O(1)$	$O(N)$

Because each of these representations leads to a $O(N)$ combined time for the search-and-insert operation, neither data structure is ideal for the task of maintaining a sorted list. It would be wonderful if there were some data structure that combined the search properties of a sorted array with the insertion properties of a linked list. Such a structure does in fact exist. To figure out what it might look like, it helps to start with the linked-list arrangement and think about its shortcomings.

To give yourself a more concrete sense of the differences between the array and linked-list representations of a sorted collection of data, imagine that the collection you are working with consists of the names of the seven dwarves from Walt Disney's *Snow White,* and that you want to keep those names in alphabetical order. In an array, the names would be laid out like this:

Bashful	Doc	Dopey	Grumpy	Happy	Sleepy	Sneezy
0	1	2	3	4	5	6

In this array representation, binary search is easy to implement because you can find the index of the middle element by dividing the length of the array by 2. The situation, however, is different in the linked-list form, which has the following conceptual structure:

In this representation, there is no way to find the middle element except by following the links in the chain.

   The problem with the linked-list representation—at least in terms of implementing the binary search operation—is that the list contains no reference pointer to the center element. But what if it did? As a thought experiment, try to imagine what happens if you change the representation of the linked list so that the reference pointer marks the middle of the list rather than its beginning. In this example, the reference pointer that represents the entire list would point to **Grumpy** instead of **Bashful**, like this:

In making this change, it is also necessary to reverse the direction of the first three arrows so that the elements **Bashful**, **Doc**, and **Dopey** remain connected to the structure. More significantly, the element representing **Grumpy** is now associated with *two* pointers, one that points to a list of the elements that come before **Grumpy** in the alphabet, and one that points to the list of names that follow it.

   This strategy, while tantalizing in certain respects, only begins to solve the problem. In this diagram, it is now easy to find the center of the entire list, since the pointer has shifted to indicate the appropriate element. Binary search, however, is a recursive divide-and-conquer strategy that makes it necessary to find not only the central element of the original list, but the center of the sublists on each side. The solution to this problem is simply to apply this same transformation recursively, so that every sublist begins in the middle and proceeds in both directions. Applying this strategy to the list of the seven dwarves results in the structure

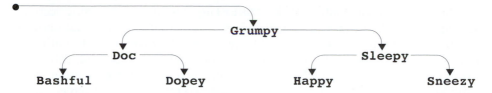

At each level, this structure branches to form two smaller structures, which are in turn decomposed in precisely the same way. In computer science, this type of structure is called a **binary tree.** In a binary tree such as the one represented here, each individual element is called a **node.** The topmost node in a tree is called the **root** of the tree. In the binary tree represented here, each node is associated with a string and a pair of object references indicating two subtrees: the subtree containing all the elements that come *before* the current node in alphabetical order and one containing the elements that come *after* this node. A binary tree that maintains this ordering property is called a **binary search tree.**

Given that storing the names of dwarves does not seem particularly useful except as an example, it makes sense to extend the simple binary search tree in a way that enables it to be used in a more practical way. The **java.util** package contains several classes that implement the **Map** interface, which provides a general dictionary-like facility that allows clients to associate a pair of objects in such a way that supplying the first object, which is called the **key,** makes it easy to find the second object, which represents the corresponding **value.** This association of a key and a value is called a **binding.**

The **Map** interface specifies quite a few methods, but the essence of a **Map** is defined by two methods:

1. **put(key, value)**, which creates a binding between **key** and **value**
2. **get(key)**, which looks up the value associated with **key**

Binary search trees provide a useful representation for implementing the **Map** interface, although other strategies exist as well. If you've been coding in Java for any length of time, it is likely that you have run across the **HashMap** class (or its earlier incarnation as **Hashtable**), which uses an algorithm called *hashing* to create the internal association. Although it is used less often, the **java.util** package also includes a **TreeMap** class that provides the same functionality using an implementation based on a more sophisticated version of binary trees. The goal for the remainder of this section is to develop a **BSTMap** class that offers a partial implementation of the **Map** interface based on the simple formulation of binary search trees presented in the earlier paragraphs. The **BSTMap** class differs from the more general map class in two respects. First, it implements only the **put** and **get** methods and not the other methods specified by the **Map** interface. Second, it assumes that the keys in the map are always of type **String**. These changes reduce the generality of the class, but simplify the presentation considerably.

As in the implementation of the **CLString** class in the preceding section, the code for the **BSTMap** class must include an internal structure that permits recursive operations on the tree used to represent the map. That definition is similar to the definition of a **CharCell** in the earlier example, but differs in two important respects. The obvious difference is that the representation of an individual node in the binary tree must include two references to subtrees rather than the single reference that is sufficient for the linked list. The more subtle change arises from the fact that the intended semantics of a **BSTMap**—for reasons that will be outlined later in this section—are far easier to implement if the subtrees are represented using the **BSTMap** class itself, rather than the internal class used for an individual node. These considerations suggest the following definition for the private **BSTNode** class:

```
class BSTNode {
    String key;
    Object value;
    BSTMap left, right;
}
```

Each **BSTMap** object includes a reference to a **BSTNode** that constitutes the root of that tree. That reference is maintained in an instance variable called **root**.

Although the primary goal of this section is to implement the methods **put** and **get**, it is useful to look first at a somewhat simpler method that offers some insight into how one might use recursion to manipulate a binary search tree. It would be convenient—for debugging reasons, if nothing else—to include as part of the definition of **BSTMap** a method

```
public void listBindings(PrintStream out)
```

that lists the bindings of keys and values that currently exist for the **BSTMap** to the **PrintStream** supplied as the argument **out**.

As a concrete illustration, imagine that you wanted to define a **BSTMap** that would translate the two-letter postal abbreviations of states into their full names. The following code creates such a map and sets up the abbreviations of the four states whose names begin with **A**:

```
BSTMap map = new BSTMap();
map.put("AL", "Alabama");
map.put("AK", "Alaska");
map.put("AZ", "Arizona");
map.put("AR", "Arkansas");
```

To test whether your **BSTMap** implementation is working, you could call

```
map.listBindings(getWriter());
```

where **getWriter** is a method that returns a **PrintWriter** to the program console. At this point you, would hope to see the following:

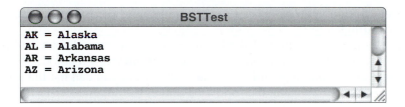

The output is sorted in alphabetical order by key, even though the entries were inserted into the tree in alphabetical order by the full name of the state.

The requirement that the output appear in alphabetical order may seem to represent a complication, particularly if you consider how this tree is represented internally. Inserting the four state abbreviations in the specified order results in a binary search tree with the following structure:

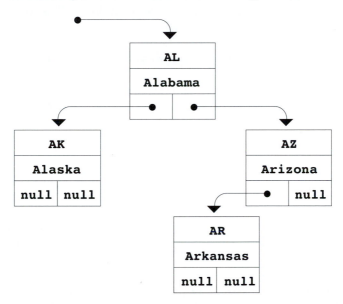

The first item to appear in the list of bindings is the binding of the abbreviation **"AK"** to **"Alaska"**, which does not occur at the root of the tree. How can the **listBindings** method know where to start?

The answer to this question lies in coding the **listBindings** method so that its structure parallels that of the data. To do so, it makes sense to start by observing that a binary search tree must be either

1. An empty tree with **null** as its root

2. A node preceded and followed by a binary search tree

This definition closely parallels the informal recursive definition of a string from the preceding section, except, of course, that each node in the binary search tree contains two subtrees rather than a single recursive instance as in the case of strings.

The recursive definition of the binary search tree provides an outline for recursive operations on a tree, such as the **listBindings** method. If a tree is empty, there are no bindings to list. For any other tree, you can list the bindings in alphabetical order by using the following strategy:

1. Recursively listing the bindings in the left subtree
2. Listing the binding specified by the root node
3. Recursively listing the bindings in the right subtree

Because the key in the root node is guaranteed to occur alphabetically after the keys in the left subtree and before the keys in the right subtree, this recursive strategy will produce a correctly ordered list of bindings. The code, moreover, follows directly from the recursive outline:

```
public void listBindings(PrintStream out) {
    if (root != null) {
        root.left.listBindings(out);
        out.println(root.key + " = " + root.value);
        root.right.listBindings(out);
    }
}
```

The **get** method for the **BSTMap** class uses a similar strategy. Consider the possibilities that arise when one calls **get** with a particular key. The first possibility is that the tree is empty, which means that the key is not present. According to its specification in the **Map** interface, **get** should return **null** in this case. But what if the tree has at least one node? In this case, there are three possibilities:

1. The key you're looking for might match the key in the current node. In this case, **get** should return the value in that node.
2. The key you're looking for might come earlier in the alphabet than the key in the current node. In this case, the key—if it is present at all in the tree— must occur in the left subtree, where it can be found by recursion.
3. The key you're looking for might come later in the alphabet than the key in the current node. This case is symmetric to the previous one and again can be solved by recursion, this time using the right subtree.

The code necessary to implement this three-case strategy looks like this:

```
public Object get(String key) {
   if (root == null) {
      return null;
   } else {
      int cmp = key.compareTo(root.key);
      if (cmp == 0) {
         return root.value;
      } else if (cmp < 0) {
         return root.left.get(key);
      } else {
         return root.right.get(key);
      }
   }
}
```

The remaining method in the simplified implementation of **BSTMap** is **put**, which has almost the same form as the **get** method. The recursive part is completely analogous, since the process of finding the appropriate node in the tree is exactly the same for the two methods. The difference lies primarily in the simple case. When **get** encounters an empty tree—either initially or as part of the recursive subdivision—it simply returns **null** to indicate that the key is not present in the tree. The **put** method, on the other hand, must create such an entry if it is not there. Given the structure chosen to represent a **BSTMap**, handling the case of an empty tree is easy. If **put** is called on a **BSTMap** object whose root is **null**, all it needs to do is create a new node with the specified key and value and then make that node the new root of the tree. The complete code for the **put** method therefore looks like this:

```
public void put(String key, Object value) {
   if (root == null) {
      root = new BSTNode();
      root.key = key;
      root.value = value;
      root.left = new BSTMap();
      root.right = new BSTMap();
   } else {
      int cmp = key.compareTo(root.key);
      if (cmp == 0) {
         root.value = value;
      } else if (cmp < 0) {
         root.left.put(key, value);
      } else {
         root.right.put(key, value);
      }
   }
}
```

This code is complicated enough to call for an example. Suppose that you wanted to add the next state abbreviation to an existing binary search tree containing entries for the four states whose names begin with **A**. The binary search tree at this point has the following internal structure:

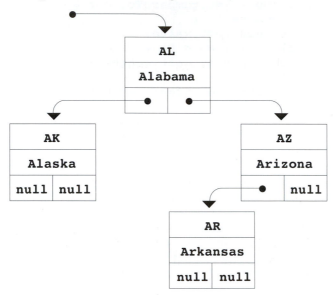

What happens to this tree if you call **map.put("CA", "California")**?

The first step in the process is to compare the key **"CA"** to the key in the root node of the binary search tree. Because **"CA"** comes after **"AL"** in the alphabet, the node with **"CA"** as its key, if it exists, must be in the right subtree. Thus, the first recursive call repeats the **put** operation in the simpler subtree that looks like this:

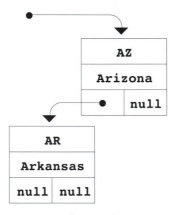

As before, the initial step consists of comparing **"CA"** to the current key and finding that the node with **"CA"** as its key must again lie in the right subtree. Here, however, that right subtree is listed in the diagram as having the value `null`. Before tracing the next level of the recursion, however, it pays to be careful about the exact structure. The subtrees in the private class **BSTNode** were deliberately defined to be of type **BSTMap** rather than **BSTNode**, which means that an additional level of object reference is involved. The **null** that appears in the diagram is really the **root** field of a new **BSTNode**, which makes it possible to replace that value with a new node containing the new key and value. After the new node has been inserted, the updated tree looks like this:

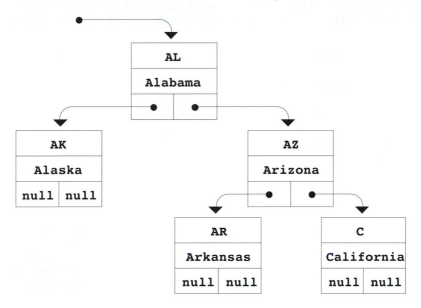

Stepping through the code for **put** makes it clear why the definition of a **BSTNode** had to include the additional level of object reference. If **BSTNode** had been defined analogously to **CharCell** in the **CLString** example from the preceding section, it would be impossible to implement the simple case of the **put** method in the straightforward way shown in the code. The **null** reference suffices to indicate the absence of a node at some point in the tree but provides no data field to which one could assign a new value. Defining the subtrees using **BSTMap** ensures that the simple case has a place to store the new node.

The discovery that the binary search tree mechanism requires an additional level of object reference brings up an interesting question: why was that additional level of reference not needed in the case of the **CLString** class? The answer lies in the fact that the two classes differ in an important respect. The **CLString** class, like the **String** class that it seeks to emulate, is immutable in the sense that no methods in the class change the internal structure. The **BSTMap** class, by contrast, does not share this property. The **put** method is useful only if it can change the underlying structure of the tree.

So that you can see how the pieces of the implementation fit together, the complete code for the **BSTMap** class appears in Figure 10-2.

Figure 10-2. The BSTMap class

```
/* Class: BSTMap */
/**
 * This class provides a partial implementation of the
 * Map interface based on binary search trees. The
 * defining feature of a binary search tree is that the
 * key value in its root node is greater than the keys
 * in its left subtree and less than those to the right.
 */

public class BSTMap {

/* Constructor: BSTMap() */
/**
 * Creates an empty binary search tree.
 */
   public BSTMap() {
      root = null;
   }

/* Method: put(key, value) */
/**
 * Creates a binding between the specified key and the
 * associated value. If a node for this key already
 * exists in this tree, the new value replaces the old
 * one. If the key is not present, the put method creates
 * a new node at the appropriate position in the tree.
 */
   public void put(String key, Object value) {
      if (root == null) {
         root = new BSTNode();
         root.key = key;
         root.value = value;
         root.left = new BSTMap();
         root.right = new BSTMap();
      } else {
         int cmp = key.compareTo(root.key);
         if (cmp == 0) {
            root.value = value;
         } else if (cmp < 0) {
            root.left.put(key, value);
         } else {
            root.right.put(key, value);
         }
      }
   }
```

continued ☞

Figure 10-2. The BSTMap class (continued)

```java
/* Method: get(key) */
/**
 * Returns the binding associated with the specified key.
 * If no such value exists, get returns null.
 */
   public Object get(String key) {
       if (root == null) {
          return null;
       } else {
          int cmp = key.compareTo(root.key);
          if (cmp == 0) {
             return root.value;
          } else if (cmp < 0) {
             return root.left.get(key);
          } else {
             return root.right.get(key);
          }
       }
   }

/* Method: listBindings(out) */
/**
 * Lists the bindings in this map in alphabetical order,
 * using the specified PrintStream to display the output.
 */
   public void listBindings(PrintStream out) {
       if (root != null) {
          root.left.listBindings(out);
          out.println(root.key + " = " + root.value);
          root.right.listBindings(out);
       }
   }

/* Private state */
   private BSTNode root;
}

/* Private class: BSTNode */
/**
 * This class provides the structure definition necessary
 * to store individual nodes in the binary search tree.
 */
class BSTNode {
   String key;
   Object value;
   BSTMap left, right;
}
```

10.3 Expression Trees

In addition to offering a computationally efficient mechanism for maintaining sorted collections of data, tree structures have many useful applications in computer science. One of the most important arises in the design and implementation of compilers, which are responsible for translating statements in a programming language into a form more easily handled by the computer itself. The process of compilation consists of translating statements in a human-readable programming language into an internal form called **machine language** while preserving the semantics of the program.

As an illustration, consider the Java expression

To translate this expression into machine language, the compiler must first determine whether it follows the rules for Java expressions and, if so, construct an internal representation of the expression that keeps track of what values are involved in the expression and the order in which the operators need to be executed to determine the proper value. The process of checking the syntax of an expression and constructing the internal form is called **parsing.**

The output of the parsing phase of a compiler is typically a recursive structure called a **parse tree.** The parse tree for the sample expression would look something like this:

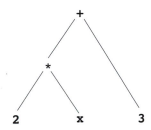

The structure of the tree shows that the expression is the sum of two values, the first of which is the product of the constant **2** and the variable **x**, and the second of which is the constant **3**.

Although the example offers some intuition into what a parse tree for expressions might contain, it is important to develop a more formal definition for an expression before trying to define its representation in Java. Because expressions often contain subexpressions, the definition for an expression is naturally recursive. The simple cases are **constants,** such as the integers **2** and **3** in the example, and **variables,** as illustrated by the symbol **x**. More complex expressions are formed by applying operators to join simpler subexpressions. For the purposes of this discussion, the set of operators will be limited to the familiar arithmetic operators **+**, **-**, *****, and **/**. Expressions formed by applying an operator to two subexpressions will be called **compound** expressions.

The fact that these three classes—constants, variables, and compounds— are all expressions suggests that these classes form an inheritance hierarchy that looks like this:

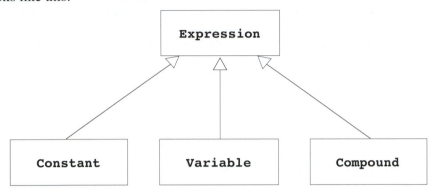

This diagram indicates that the classes **Constant**, **Variable**, and **Compound** are each subclasses of the more general **Expression** class. Moreover, by convention, the class name **Expression** is in italics to show that **Expression** is an abstract class, which means that there are no objects of class **Expression** *per se,* but only of the concrete subclasses. (The diagram also shows that **Compound** is an abstract class, but the reasons for this design decision will be deferred until the **Compound** class is considered in more detail later in this section.)

Even though **Expression** is an abstract class, it is still appropriate to define methods at this level of the hierarchy as long as those methods apply to all the subclasses. Moreover, if there is a method that each of the subclasses must implement to be a legitimate expression, but which each subclass is likely to implement in its own way, the **Expression** class can mark that method as **abstract**, which enables the Java compiler to check whether each subclass implements that method. The **Expression** class shown in Figure 10-3 defines two abstract methods, as follows:

1. An **eval()** method, which evaluates the expression to return an integer.

2. An **unparse(out)** method, which displays a human-readable version of the expression, using the **PrintStream** object specified by **out**.

The individual subclasses must define their own implementations for each of these methods.

The two simple cases—**Constant** and **Variable**—are easy to define. They appear in Figures 10-4 and 10-5, respectively. For both classes, the definitions of **eval** and **unparse** are nonrecursive because these subclasses represent the simple case that terminates the recursive process.

Figure 10-3. The Expression class

```
/* Class: Expression */
/**
 * This abstract class specifies the behavior that all
 * objects of type Expression must implement. Because
 * Expression is an abstract class, only the concrete
 * subclasses of Expression can actually be constructed.
 */

public abstract class Expression {

/* Default constructor: Expression */
/**
 * Creates a default expression. Java requires that
 * this empty constructor exist so that the subclass
 * constructors can create the common superclass.
 */
   protected Expression() { }

/* Abstract method: eval() */
/**
 * Evaluates an expression to return an integer. Each
 * Expression subclass must implement this method.
 */
   public abstract int eval();

/* Abstract method: unparse(out) */
/**
 * Writes out a human-readable version of the expression
 * to the specified PrintStream.
 */
   public abstract void unparse(PrintStream out);

}
```

Figure 10-4. The Constant class

```
/* Class: Constant */
/**
 * This expression subclass represents an integer
 * constant.
 */

public class Constant extends Expression {

/* Constructor: Constant(value) */
/**
 * Creates a constant expression with the specified value.
 */
   public Constant(int value) {
      this.value = value;
   }

/* Method: eval() */
/**
 * Evaluates an expression to return an integer. For
 * the Constant class, the result is simply the value.
 */
   public int eval() {
      return value;
   }

/* Method: unparse(out) */
/**
 * Writes a human-readable version of the expression
 * to the specified PrintStream. For a Constant, this
 * representation is simply the value.
 */
   public void unparse(PrintStream out) {
      out.print(value);
   }

/* Private state */
   private int value;

}
```

Figure 10-5. The Variable class

```
/* Class: Variable */
/**
 * This expression subclass represents a variable.
 */

public class Variable extends Expression {

/* Constructor: Variable(name) */
/**
 * Creates a variable with the specified name.
 */
   public Variable(String name) {
      this.name = name;
   }

/* Method: eval() */
/**
 * Evaluates an expression to return an integer. For
 * the Variable class, the result is the stored value.
 */
   public int eval() {
      return value;
   }

/* Method: unparse(out) */
/**
 * Writes out a human-readable version of the expression
 * to the specified PrintStream. For a Variable, this
 * representation is simply the name.
 */
   public void unparse(PrintStream out) {
      out.print(name);
   }

/* Method: assignValue(value) */
/**
 * Assigns a new value to a variable.
 */
   public void assignValue(int value) {
      this.value = value;
   }

/* Private state */

   private String name;
   private int value;

}
```

The **Compound** expression subclass is more interesting. In this case, the value returned by **eval** depends on the operator. Although it would be possible to define the **Compound** class so that it made an explicit test for each operator and then performed the appropriate calculation, such a strategy would not take advantage of the power of object-oriented programming. It is cleaner to define each operator as a specific subclass of **Compound** that knows how to apply its operation. Thus, the **Compound** subclass shown in Figure 10-6 is itself an abstract class that delegates the evaluation of each operator to an **apply** method, which is defined separately for each subclass. The definition of **apply** for the multiplication operator *, for example, is simply

```
public int apply(int lhs, int rhs) {
    return lhs * rhs;
}
```

The recursive aspect of the evaluation process lies in the definition of **eval** in the **Compound** class, which looks like this:

```
public int eval() {
    return apply(lhs.eval(), rhs.eval());
}
```

The effect of this method can be described in English as follows:

1. Evaluate the **lhs** and **rhs** subexpressions using recursive calls to **eval**.

2. Invoke the **apply** operator for this class to calculate the result.

The implementation for **unparse** in the **Compound** class is similarly recursive, as you can see from the code in Figure 10-6.

One interesting thing to note about the expression tree example is that none of the methods actually follows the paradigmatic form for recursive methods, which begins with a test for a simple case. There are, in fact, no tests of any kind anywhere in the code that implements expression trees. The determination of whether a particular case is simple or complex is implicit in the inheritance hierarchy of the subclasses. A simple case constitutes having in hand one of the simple subclasses, **Constant** or **Variable**; recursion comes up only if the expression is a **Compound**.

Exercises

10-1. Starting with the code in Figure 10-1, rewrite the methods **length**, **concat**, **toString**, and **toCLString** so that they operate iteratively without using recursion.

Figure 10-6. The Compound class

```
/* Class: Compound */
/**
 * This expression subclass represents a compound
 * expression consisting of an operator and two
 * subexpressions.
 */

public abstract class Compound extends Expression {

/* Constructor: Compound(op, lhs, rhs) */
/**
 * Creates a compound expression that combines the two
 * operands with the specified operator.
 */
   public Compound(char op, Expression lhs, Expression rhs) {
      this.op = op;
      this.lhs = lhs;
      this.rhs = rhs;
   }

/* Method: eval() */
/**
 * Evaluates an expression to return an integer. For
 * the Compound class, the result is defined in terms
 * of the apply method, which differs for each operator.
 */
   public int eval() {
      return apply(lhs.eval(), rhs.eval());
   }

/* Method: unparse(out) */
/**
 * Writes out a human-readable version of the expression
 * to the specified PrintStream. For a Compound, this
 * method is implemented recursively.
 */
   public void unparse(PrintStream out) {
      out.print("(");
      lhs.unparse(out);
      out.print(" " + op + " ");
      rhs.unparse(out);
      out.print(")");
   }
```

continued ☞

Figure 10-6. The Compound class (continued)

```
/* Abstract method: apply(lhs, rhs) */
/**
 * Implements the meaning of a specific operator. Each
 * Compound subclass defines its own apply method to
 * carry out the computation for that operator.
 */
   public abstract int apply(int lhs, int rhs);

/* Private state */

   private char op;
   private Expression lhs, rhs;

}


/* Private class: AddCompound */
/**
 * This class defines the Compound subclass that
 * represents addition.
 */

class AddCompound extends Compound {

/* Constructor: AddCompound(lhs, rhs) */
/**
 * Creates a new Compound expression that uses the +
 * operator.
 */
   public AddCompound(Expression lhs, Expression rhs) {
      super('+', lhs, rhs);
   }

/* Method: apply(lhs, rhs) */
/**
 * Implements the meaning of the + operator.
 */
   public int apply(int lhs, int rhs) {
      return lhs + rhs;
   }
}
```

This file must also contain similar class definitions for the other operators.

10-2. Suppose that someone has added the following method definition to the **CLString** class in Figure 10-1:

```
private String mystery(CharCell list) {
   if (list == null) {
      return "";
   } else {
      return mystery(list.link) + list.ch;
   }
}
```

What does the method **mystery** do? Can you duplicate the effect of this method without using recursion?

10-3. Extend the definition of **CLString** so that it also implements the following methods from the standard **String** class:

```
public char charAt(int index)

public int indexOf(int ch)

public CLString substring(int begin, int end)
```

10-4. As presented in section 10.1, the **CLString** class is extremely inefficient in its use of space, since each character requires enough storage to hold not only the character but also a reference to the next cell in the linked list, which presumably requires even more space than the character does. To reduce this overhead, it is possible to define strings so that the chaining is done on the basis of character blocks rather than individual characters. Design a new string-like class that stores more than one character within each cell. Discuss the effect that this new representation has on the efficiency of the standard methods in the **String** class, along with any design tradeoffs you anticipate.

10-5. It is also possible to represent the internal value of a string by using a tree structure instead of a linked list. The advantage of doing so is that the **concat** operation can then operate in constant time, although the cost is ultimately reflected in less efficient implementations of several of the other methods.

To see how this representation might work, suppose that you have defined a new string-like class in which the simple-case representation is simply the traditional Java **String**, but which also supports a representation consisting of two strings concatenated together. For example, if you had two simple strings representing **"ABC"** and **"DEF"**, concatenating these two values should produce a pair that looks more or less like this:

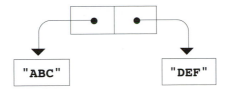

Design a **TreeString** class that uses this underlying representation. Your implementation should include the same public methods defined in the text: a **TreeString** constructor and the methods **length**, **concat**, and **toString**.

10-6. In the discussion of the complexity order of insertion using a binary tree, the statement includes the disclaimer that the input values must be distributed in a reasonably random order. What would happen if an overzealous clerk sorted a large batch of entries by hand and then fed them into the binary tree insertion mechanism in that order?

10-7. Diagram the tree that results if the following keys are inserted into an empty binary search tree in the specified order:

> **H, He, Li, Be, B, C, N, O, F, Ne**

10-8. The **depth** of a binary tree is defined to be the length of the longest path that runs from the root of the tree to one of the terminal nodes. Add a method **treeDepth()** to the **BSTMap** class that returns the depth of the tree used to store the map.

10-9. Many of the electronic calculators produced in the early 1970s required the user to put the data in **reverse Polish notation,** in which the operands are written first, followed by the operator. For example, the expression in conventional algebraic notation

> **2 * x + 3**

becomes

> **2 x * 3 +**

in reverse Polish notation. Using **unparse** as a model, add a new method **unparseRPN(out)** to the **Expression** class that displays an expression tree in reverse Polish form.

Implementing Recursion

Never trust to general impressions, my boy, but concentrate yourself upon details.
> —Sir Arthur Conan Doyle, *A Case of Identity*, 1891

Up to this point, this book has been concerned with developing a strategy for recursive programming based on a high-level understanding of the underlying mechanism. For the person who shares with Sherlock Holmes a desire to reduce a problem to its smallest details, it is important to consider the implementation of recursion from a more intimate perspective.

The discussion of the Tower of Hanoi puzzle in Chapter 5 offered a conceptual model for the implementation of recursion using a stack of index cards to manage the necessary bookkeeping operations. When faced with a recursive implementation, a computer system must keep track of the same sort of information in its internal storage. More specifically, the computer must keep track of the following information for every method call:

1. The values of all local variables for this method, making sure that the new set of values do not interfere with those in any as-yet-unfinished call

2. The point in the program at which this method call was made so that execution can continue from the proper point when this method returns.

What makes this bookkeeping difficult is the fact that the computer must maintain this information for each level in the recursive decomposition simultaneously. Calling a method introduces a new environment that temporarily supersedes the preceding one. When that procedure returns, the old environment is restored.

11.1 The Control Stack Model

To keep track of this state information through a sequence of method calls, most computers make use of specialized instructions defined in the machine hardware to implement a structure called the **control stack.** Internally, the control stack consists of an array of consecutive memory locations associated

165

with a stack pointer register (called **SP** in the remainder of this section) that points to the last item entered on the stack. In most modern hardware architectures, the control stack starts at the highest available addresses in memory and grows toward lower addresses. Because memory is usually diagrammed with the lowest address numbers on top, stack diagrams usually show stacks growing upward from the bottom of the figure (highest addresses) to the top (lowest addresses). The diagrams in this chapter follow this convention and further assume that the highest memory location—and therefore the first element in the control stack—is at the machine address 9999.

Modern computer systems typically include several built-in instructions for manipulating the control stack, of which the most fundamental are traditionally called **PUSH** and **POP**. The **PUSH** instruction takes a value and adds it to the top of the stack. If you start with an empty stack and then push the value 3, the stack looks like this:

Pushing the value 5 results in the configuration

The **POP** operation returns the most recent value pushed on the stack (in this case, the 5) and adjusts the **SP** register to indicate the next most recent value. Conventionally, the value 5 is not actually removed from storage, but is no longer accessible:

In a stack, the last value pushed is always the first value popped. For this reason, a stack is sometimes referred to as a "last-in/first-out" storage mechanism, which is often abbreviated as **LIFO.** Significantly, this last-in/first-out discipline is precisely the behavior of method calls. The last method called is always the first method that returns. This similarity between the behavior of method calls and the fundamental stack operations is what makes stacks ideal as a data structure for keeping track of the method calls in a program.

Whenever a method call occurs in the course of executing a program, the first step in the operation is to evaluate each of the arguments and push them on the control stack. Thus, if you were to call the **moveTower** method from Chapter 5 with the arguments

```
moveTower(3, "A", "B", "C")
```

the evaluation of the method call would begin by pushing each of the arguments on the control stack, which would lead to the following configuration (assuming that the stack was initially empty):

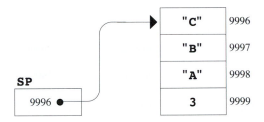

The next step in calling a method is to transfer control to the body of the method in such a way that it is later possible to return to the point at which the call was made. This operation is usually implemented by a single built-in machine instruction, typically named **CALL**. The **CALL** instruction does two things. First, it pushes the address of the instruction following the **CALL** on the control stack. Because this address is the location from which the program should continue when the method returns, it is known as the **return address.** For example, if the **CALL** instruction in the machine-language version of the program happens to be located at address 536 in memory, executing that **CALL** instruction pushes 537 on the stack as the return address, as illustrated by the following diagram:

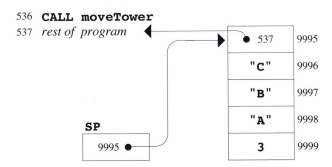

The second part of the **CALL** instruction operation is simply to transfer control to the procedure itself. The fact that the return address is stored on the control stack means that the program can eventually get back to where it left off.

If you compare the values on the stack with those on the first index card shown in the informal view of recursive implementation on page 66, you will quickly notice that they contain the same information. The region of the stack that is assigned to a particular method call is known as a **stack frame** and is analogous to a single index card in the informal model. As long as a particular method call is active, the references to its local variables always refer to the contents of the appropriate memory location in the current stack frame. At the machine level, these memory addresses are referred to in terms of their offset from the position of the stack pointer, but for the human reader it helps to label the current frame with the names of the corresponding variables. The contents of the labeled stack frame look like this:

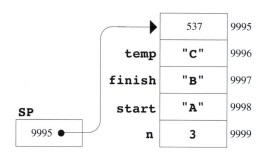

As an example, let's consider what happens when you start to execute the body of the **moveTower** method after this initial call. To refresh your memory, the code for **moveTower** looks like this:

```
void moveTower(int n, char start, char finish,
                                   char temp) {
    if (n == 1) {
        println(start + " -> " + finish);
    } else {
        moveTower(n - 1, start, temp, finish);
        println(start + " -> " + finish);
        moveTower(n - 1, temp, finish, start);
    }
}
```

When the computer begins executing the body of the method, it must find the value of the variable **n** by looking at the appropriate cell in the current stack frame, which shows that the value of **n** is currently 3. Control therefore passes to the **else** branch of the **if** statement, which begins with the following recursive call to **moveTower**:

```
moveTower(n - 1, start, temp, finish);
```

The recursive call is treated exactly like the original one: the arguments are evaluated and pushed on the stack, followed by the return address. If this instruction is at location 563, the return address will be 564, and the control stack prior to starting the recursive invocation of **moveTower** will look like this:

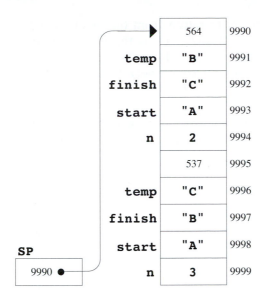

The new stack frame looks very much like the previous one, with different values for the arguments. Moreover, the old values for the original call still remain in an earlier stack frame. The values in that frame are not used until control returns to that level, when they will once again become available.

You can, of course, continue this analysis to any depth you choose. If you continued from this point, for example, the next step would be yet another recursive call to **moveTower**, this time with **n** equal to 1. At that point, the **if** statement discovers that a simple case has been reached, making it possible to complete the solution with no additional recursive calls.

Returning from a method consists of the following steps:

1. Adjusting the stack pointer so that it points to the previous frame
2. Transferring control back to the return address saved on the stack

Suppose, for example, that the computer has completed the entire second-level call to

```
moveTower(2, "A", "C", "B");
```

and has therefore already produced the output

The program is now set to return from the position shown in the last stack diagram. The top item on the stack is the return address 564, which is the address of the instruction that follows the first recursive call in the body of **moveTower**. The return from **moveTower** therefore consists of

1. Popping the return address
2. Discarding the arguments on the stack to restore the previous stack frame
3. Jumping to the return address popped in step 1 and continuing on from there

At this point, the control stack again looks like

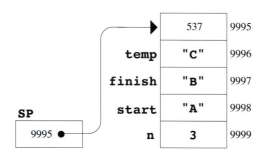

which means that the variables again have the values appropriate to the original stack frame.

11.2 Simulating Recursion

When you are using a high-level language like Java, the stack operations described in the previous section are carried out automatically, and you can remain blissfully ignorant of the details. In part, the attractiveness of recursion lies in the fact that much of this complexity is hidden away, which makes it possible for you to concentrate on the algorithm itself.

At the same time, it is possible—though tedious—to perform the stack operations explicitly and thereby simulate the recursive operation. If you are using an older language that does not support recursion (such as FORTRAN), defining an explicit control stack is often the only way to code a recursive algorithm. And even though there is no need to simulate recursion in modern languages like Java, doing so can sometimes provide a more precise understanding of the underlying mechanics.

At one level, the simplest way to simulate recursion is to model the stack in much the same way that the underlying machine does, pushing the values of each argument individually prior to a method call and popping those values off when the method returns. Such a strategy, however, does not take advantage of Java's data structuring capabilities. Since Java makes it possible to represent structures that are more complex than individual stack entries, it seems preferable to simulate recursion in Java at a somewhat higher level of abstraction. For instance, one strategy that seems particularly appropriate is to define a Java class that represents a complete stack frame for the Tower of Hanoi problem. Once you have defined such a class, you can implement the Tower of Hanoi solution in a way that mirrors its conceptual structure.

For the most part, the elements of a stack frame are easy to represent as a Java class. The only components that actually appear in the index-card diagrams from Chapter 5 are the parameters, which you can represent as instance variables of the private class that models each stack frame from the Tower of Hanoi puzzle. Thus, the definition of the stack frame class will look something like this:

```
class Frame {
    int n;
    char start, finish, temp;
}
```

This definition, however, is missing an important component. If you look at the stack traces in the preceding section, you will discover that each call to **moveTower** pushes *five* values on the stack, only four of which are included in the frame. The missing item is the return address, which is difficult to represent explicitly in Java, because modern high-level languages deliberately hide such low-level details from the programmer. Even so, you need to find some way to remember where to return from each call to **moveTower** because such bookkeeping is essential to the recursive operation.

There are many strategies you could use to simulate return addresses in Java. One approach is to divide the body of the method into a series of individual steps and then identify each of the steps by an integer value. The idea behind this process is illustrated by the following piece of the **moveTower** code, which is annotated with position numbers to represent various points of progress through the evaluation of the recursive case:

```
① →  moveTower(n - 1, start, temp, finish);
② →  printLine(start + " -> " + finish);
③ →  moveTower(n - 1, temp, finish, start);
④ →
```

The four numbered arrows at the left mark each of the possible positions during the execution of the recursive case of **moveTower**. If you use an integer variable to keep track of the current position in this section of the code, you can save and restore that value in much the same manner as you do a return address. The value would always be 1 at the beginning of a recursive call and 4 just before the call returns.

At the hardware level, the register that keeps track of the current instruction in the program is usually called the **PC**, which stands for **program counter.** Because the integer values indicating the various positions in the code correspond in function to the low-level addresses stored in the **PC**, it makes sense to add a **pc** field to the definition of the **Frame** class to ensure that the program knows how to proceed after returning from a simulated method call. The class definition for the **Frame** class appears in Figure 11-1.

The complete code for a solution to the Tower of Hanoi puzzle without explicit recursion appears in Figure 11-2. If, after having studied the previous chapters, you still find the process of recursion confusing, it might help to go through this implementation carefully to make sure you can follow its internal operation.

Exercises

11-1. Apply the strategy used in this chapter to simulate the recursive structure of other examples from the earlier chapters, such as the **fib** function from Chapter 3 or the **listPermutations** method from Chapter 6.

11-2. The implementation of recursion used in this chapter was chosen deliberately to correspond as closely as possible to the control stack

Figure 11-1 . Class used to represent a stack frame for the Tower of Hanoi

```
/* Private class: Frame */
/**
 * This class collects the data needed for each recursive
 * call to moveTower.  The fields in this structure are
 * precisely those that would be stored in a stack frame.
 */
class Frame {

/* Constructor to create a Frame from its components */
    Frame(int n, char start, char finish, char temp, int pc) {
        this.n = n;
        this.start = start;
        this.finish = finish;
        this.temp = temp;
        this.pc = pc;
    }

/* Fields accessible to the moveTower code */
    int n;
    char start, finish, temp;
    int pc;
}
```

Figure 11-2. Method to simulate the recursive Tower of Hanoi solution

```
/* Method: moveTower(n, start, finish, temp) */
/**
 * Writes out the moves in the Tower of Hanoi puzzle
 * necessary to move a tower of size n from the start
 * spire to the finish spire, using the remaining
 * spire for temporary storage.  This implementation
 * uses a stack to simulate the recursive operation.
 */
    void moveTower(int n, char start, char finish, char temp) {
        Stack stack = new Stack();
        stack.push(new Frame(n, start, finish, temp, 0));
        int pc = 1;
        while (pc != 0) {
            Frame cf = (Frame) stack.peek();
            if (cf.n == 1) {
                println(cf.start + " -> " + cf.finish);
                pc = 4;
            } else {
                switch (pc) {
                  case 1:
                    stack.push(new Frame(cf.n - 1, cf.start,
                                         cf.temp, cf.finish,
                                         pc + 1));
                    pc = 1;
                    break;
                  case 2:
                    println(cf.start + " -> " + cf.finish);
                    pc = 3;
                    break;
                  case 3:
                    stack.push(new Frame(cf.n - 1, cf.temp,
                                         cf.finish, cf.start,
                                         pc + 1));
                    pc = 1;
                    break;
                }
            }
            if (pc == 4) {
                pc = ((Frame) stack.pop()).pc;
            }
        }
    }
}
```

model used by the computer. You can, however, use other strategies to simulate recursion. For many applications, you can maintain a stack of unfinished subtasks without going through the effort necessary to model the control stack in detail.

To get a sense of how this strategy might work, imagine that you are trying to use this approach to solve the Tower of Hanoi problem. In that problem, every subtask can be defined by four pieces of information: the number of disks, the start needle, the finish needle, and the temporary needle. You can easily define a **HanoiTask** class to encapsulate this information in a single object in much the same way that the **Frame** class defined in this chapter encapsulates the information in a stack frame. You then create a new **Stack** object, which you might call **pendingTasks**, to keep track of the unfinished tasks. To get things started, you simply push the highest level task on the stack. For example, if your goal were to move a tower of six disks from A to B using C for temporary storage, you would execute the following call:

```
pendingTasks.push(new HanoiTask(6, "A", "B", "C"));
```

To simulate the recursion, you would then write a program that executes the following pseudocode strategy:

```
while (any tasks remain on the stack of pending tasks) {
    Pop the top task off the stack.
    if (the task represents a simple case) {
        Do whatever is necessary to solve the simple case.
    } else {
        Divide the task into its component subtasks.
        Push each subtask on the pending task stack in reverse order.
    }
}
```

For example, in the first cycle of this loop, your program would push the following subtasks on the stack:

```
new HanoiTask(5, "C", "B", "A")
new HanoiTask(1, "A", "B", "C")
new HanoiTask(5, "A", "C", "B")
```

Complete the implementation of a program that uses this strategy to simulate recursion.

Index